I'm for
ROOSEVELT

I'm for
ROOSEVELT

★ ★ ★

JOSEPH P. KENNEDY

REYNAL & HITCHCOCK

New York

CONTENTS

I'm for
ROOSEVELT

In Which the Father of Nine Children Explains What He Thinks this Election Means to Them

I

POLITICS furnishes to government its man-power, machinery, the failures of that machinery and— through an opposition—the checking system without which no man or machine will function efficiently. Politics, therefore, is, or should be, the acute concern of every citizen; and the richer his interests, whether they consist of family, a passion for individual liberty, worldly goods—or all of them—the more closely he should examine the processes of politics.

As a citizen, a business man, and a father concerned about the future of the growing generation I am particularly interested in politics. That is the excuse I offer for writing this book on the eve of a presidential election. It is at once a chart of my immediate political course and an answer to numerous friends and acquaintances who ask "How can you support Roosevelt?"

On July 3, 1934, President Roosevelt appointed me a member of the Securities and Exchange Commission, which had just been created by an Act of Congress. Within a few days the other members of the Commission elected me Chairman. Congress turned over to the new Commission the administration of the Securities Act of 1933, which required truthful disclosures in the public offering of securities, and in addition provided a comprehensive system of supervision for the organized and over-the-counter markets of this country in order to protect the investor and establish fair principles for trading in securities.

This appointment made me part of the administration, and officially I continued to be part of it until September 23, 1935. In accordance with an informal understanding I had with the President at the time of my selection, I resigned on that date, the purpose of my appointment having been accomplished and the Commission having been strongly established as a going concern. When I left the government service, the President wrote me a letter of commendation and expressed the wish that I should continue to regard myself as part of the administration.

I mention these facts so there shall be no misapprehension about my personal feelings for President Roosevelt. He has favored me with an appointment to an office of great honor and I am warmly grateful for the privilege of his intimate friendship and for the confidence in me which this appointment revealed.

Nevertheless, these personal feelings, however they may have affected my disposition to write about the President, do not constitute the occasion for my efforts or the reason for my writing. In this discussion I have attempted to be as objective and impersonal as the makeup of mankind permits.

I am rated a man of wealth, as that term is generally understood. I am the father of nine children, a fact which admits of no misunderstanding. Because of these reasons, particularly because of my family, the future of this country, immediate and remote, political and economic, is a matter which concerns me vitally. I have no political ambitions for myself or for my children and I put down these few thoughts about our President, conscious only of my concern as a father for the future of his family and my anxiety as a citizen that the facts about the President's philosophy be not lost in a fog of unworthy emotion.

I must confess to a feeling of mystification when I listen to some of the critics of President Roosevelt. Not one of these mentions the state of the nation when he first took office; no analysis is made of the economic collapse which immediately preceded the first Democratic administration since the World War. I wonder—is it convenient forgetfulness, or are these people ashamed of the thoughts they felt and expressed at the time when seemingly all values were disappearing and ruin threatened? I am not ashamed to record that in those days I felt and said I would be willing to part with half of what I had if I could be sure of keeping, under law and order, the other half. Then it seemed that I should be able to hold nothing for the protection of my family. I know that many present critics of the President spoke and felt the same way. Gratitude is a noble virtue, all the more noble because seldom found, infrequently commensurate with the benefit received and hardly of long duration.

In that time of crisis came the President, courageous, clear-headed, inspiring confidence in ourselves and in the moral and material welfare of the Nation.

Almost in an instant a night of chaos became the dawn of renewed hopes. This transformation is a matter of newspaper record. Editorials throughout the land praised "The Deliverer" who inspired a nation to rise from the depths of despair, the leader who had received a mandate from the people to reform the legal and economic order which had been proved inadequate to avert the widespread misery that afflicted all classes of citizens. I think it appropriate to reproduce here, at this time, the summary of editorial comment throughout the nation which was printed in the "Literary Digest" for March 11, 1933, as part of the leading article entitled "The New President's Call to Battle."

And now we turn to discover how the press of the country, from ocean to ocean, Republican as well as Democratic, passes judgment on this Roosevelt inaugural. And we find wide acknowledgment of its courage, its declaration of leadership, its willingness to accept responsibility, its note of high moral indignation. Criticism is but infrequently heard.

It "has the punch," bluntly says The Telegram of Portland, Maine. In Mississippi the Jackson News (Dem.) confessed to a thrill of delight when it saw Franklin Delano Roosevelt ascending Capitol Hill and carrying "on his sturdy shoulders the big stick made famous in Roosevelt tradition." In the capital city itself the Washington Post testified that "the determination to act, and to act heroically, strikes the popular chord."

"President Roosevelt," says the Seattle Times, on the Pacific Coast, "made his purpose crystal clear when he compared the nation to an army marching to battle against the foreign foe." Similarly, the Cleveland Plain Dealer (Dem.), Detroit News (Ind.), and Houston Chronicle (Dem.) admire the "fighting" qualities of the speech. The listeners to the Roosevelt inaugural were above all else struck with the fearlessness it showed, so the Providence News-Tribune (Dem.) thinks. The address, according to the Chicago Tribune (Rep.), "strikes the dominant note of courageous confidence."

But the big thing about the inaugural, in the opinion of many newspapers scattered throughout the country, is the "vigorous assertion of national leadership," as the Kansas City Star (Ind.) puts it. It is one more proof, as the Nashville Banner (Dem.) reads our history, "That, as every great epoch has called for a great leader, so never has the nation lacked the citizen to measure to the demands." The new Executive, in the words of the Republican New York Herald Tribune, speaks "Like a true leader, who realizes the difficulties before him, and faces them unafraid."

"He is a leader who means to lead," the Louisville Courier-Journal (Dem.) is convinced. The address "was well calculated to inspire confidence," in the opinion of the Republican Los Angeles Times. The inaugural speech "was the bold work of leadership that the hour demanded," insists the Norfolk Virginian-Pilot (Dem.); "its utterance has put new steel in the nation's spirit, and with that steel will conquer."

The President's program "demands the dictatorial authority he requests," reasons the Republican Boston Transcript. This is unprecedented in its implications, we are further told, but "such is the desperate temper of the people that it is welcome." With Roosevelt's purpose in this respect, similarly concludes the Minneapolis Journal

(Rep.), "he will find the country in full accord." The Macon Telegraph (Dem.) points out that by giving the new President the powers he desires and needs, "Congress can keep its hold on the governmental structure." But "if Congress fails it, the country will strongly back him in his demand for virtual war powers," opines the Dallas News (Dem.).

The people "must give President Roosevelt the support he demands," insists the Newark News (Ind.), "even to the point of submitting their lives and property to the discipline that may be necessary to bring us out of this dark hour." The Denver Post (Ind.) suggests that "giving him these dictatorial powers at the very beginning will save much time." But the Kansas City Journal Post (Rep.) argues rather differently that "the fact that he has announced his readiness to make this move may relieve Mr. Roosevelt of the necessity of making it," because it will persuade Congress in advance to coöperate.

These few examples of editorial comment demonstrate how desperate had been the nation's plight, how completely the new President had caught the imagination of our people, how grateful they were for his leadership.

But what do we now hear and witness? Those who, in the last days of President Hoover's administration, would have given half of all they possessed to save the rest, now have much more. Yet they have turned venomously on the man responsible for this change.

Let us consider this strange social manifestation of class emotion which reveals itself in hatred for the President of the United States. Who are the haters and

why do they hate? Recently a leading magazine pub-
lished an article by a competent student of current
affairs entitled "They Hate Roosevelt." Anyone who
has moved in the circles of so-called fashion and
actual wealth can testify to the truth of my contention that "hatred" is the only word that properly
defines the attitude toward Roosevelt of thousands of
men and women among the more fortunate American
classes. Theirs is not a political disagreement or
even a moral dispute. It is an unreasoning, fanatical,
blind, irrational prejudice against President Roosevelt
and his plans for a fairer national economy.

Many public men who have discussed this problem
seem to conclude that we are witnessing the strangest
hatred of history, because the most articulate
and venomous among the opposition are those
very persons whose fortunes have been repaired
through Presidential activities since March, 1933.
The usual historical or logical consequence would be
approbation for a leader from such as these. There is a
grim paradox in the cold record of a startling economic recovery among those who now advocate the
complete overthrow of the President's policies.

It certainly can be said without exaggeration that
the Chief Executive has been at pains to protect the
invested wealth of the nation. He has in every important speech, even when attacking the manifest
abuses of irresponsible wealth, made clear that he
advocates no policy of expropriation, no scheme of
confiscation. At no time has he failed to assert or
imply his belief in the essential capitalistic economy

under which America and the American system have developed.

One could add to the picture another note of irony by citing the complaint of an intelligent Socialist who, in a well-documented book, accuses President Roosevelt of masquerading as a Socialist. With great acumen he demonstrates the theory that the Socialists should oppose President Roosevelt because essentially he thinks as an aristocrat of Dutchess County should think, and acts in terms of the capitalist system that sent him to Groton, to Harvard, to Albany, and to Washington, wealthy enough to enjoy those creature comforts the lack of which so frequently drive men to Socialism and Communism.

It is a point in evidence that the President has attained a successful middle-of-the-road liberalism that wealthy and reactionary persons in our national life join with radicals in criticism.

It is to the people that the President addresses himself, and, as in Lincoln's day, I believe the people are more firm than ever in support of the President and offer their affectionate loyalty.

It is part of my belief that time will justify President Roosevelt's policies as it has vindicated the action of those hated in other days. I agree with his judgment that our economic crisis was in effect a moral crisis, and what happened in 1929 was the result of "a decade of debauch, of group selfishness . . . every man for himself and the devil take the hindmost."[1] I also sub-

[1] See also speeches by Governor Alf M. Landon of Kansas in 1933, 1934, 1935 to the same effect.

scribe to the view he reiterated recently at the Jefferson Day dinner in New York—that the national prosperity cannot be a game of see-saw with the farmers up this year and the wage-earners down, their respective positions to be reversed within the space of a few years.

Frequently during my service with the Securities and Exchange Commission I encountered issuers, underwriters, promoters, brokers, dealers, stock exchange officials and persons of all types involved in the securities business who firmly believed that the legislation of Congress in 1933 and 1934 represented devices of the devil himself. The investment business was doomed; the stock market had met up with a fatal paralysis as a result of these reforms!

Well, what happened? Instead of getting worse, business got better. I pleaded, I argued, I entreated that the thing to do was to be natural, not hysterical. Later, the more intelligent of the investment community realized that the legislation was sound, that its objectives were worthwhile, and that in the long run there would result from these reform activities great benefit to the decent people in the business. To their amazement there was an immediate gain in securities sales and trading which fair-minded men had to attribute to the Commission's inspiring restoration of the public confidence.

Regardless of the identities of those who will occupy the White House in the years to come, the American people must face problems that will require the exercise of their very best qualities of mind and soul. To solve these difficulties will require self-restraint and cooperation—the antitheses of that spirit the present malice begets.

The cause of democracy has come upon hard times in the world since 1914. Nation after nation has succumbed to dictatorships. But democracy is more than a manner of governing people. Basically it is an adventure in self-discipline. Our nation began as a democracy in that spiritual sense. Essentially, the present American system is a government which functions because of self-imposed discipline and by that I mean to include the discipline of one's emotions when selfish unrestrained passion threatens the commonweal.

The danger comes from within. I can think of no more definite symptom of this danger than the unreasoning malicious ill-will displayed by the rich and powerful against our common leader. Because I appreciate the perils arising from this hatred, and because of my abiding faith that the future happiness of America, which means to me the future happiness of my family, will best be served by the re-election of President Roosevelt, I have set down a few observations in the hope that they will assist in restoring a temperate discussion of issues.

CHAPTER .II

*In Which the Background and Philosophy of
the New Deal are Analyzed*

I

LET me first say that I do not subscribe to the
partisan view that the administration has been
without blemish. It has made many mistakes. Some I
believe to be serious and unnecessary—as for example
the tax bill of 1936 (of which more later). But history
chronicles no President whose record for even one year
was flawless. By comparison with leaders of other
days President Roosevelt will, by many fair-minded
observers, be accounted worthy of renown.

It requires no intellectual capacity to indulge in
sweeping generalizations about the "mess in Washington," or such terms as "regimentation," "exploitation," etc. I suppose it is natural for political partisanship to express itself in extreme figures of speech
and to exhaust the dictionary for superlatives that
will serve the purposes of propaganda. But such tactics do not advance the common cause. They do not
even advance the cause of the declaimer.

Intemperate opposition is not without precedent in
American history. As a people Americans are not
easily stirred to action. The spectacle must be dra-
matic. The movie is worthless unless it is at least
colossal. Social injustices may be ignored unless they
are luridly portrayed. Nevertheless if we wish to re-

gard ourselves as adult-minded, even the opposition ought to make candid confession that the ultimate objectives of President Roosevelt coincide with the essential processes of sound government.

As to the means, there are and should be differences of opinion. Even the Chief Justice of the United States has defended judicial disagreement on the highest court of the land. Only the other day he said:

"How amazing it is that in the midst of controversies on every conceivable subject, one would expect unanimity of opinion upon difficult legal questions!

"In the highest ranges of thought, in theology, philosophy and science, we find differences of view on the part of the most distinguished experts—theologians, philosophers, and scientists.

"The history of scholarship is a record of disagreements. And when we deal with questions relating to principles of law and their application, we do not suddenly rise to a stratosphere of icy certainty."

Turning now to more specific criticism of the President's policies termed the "New Deal," let us weigh them as a political philosophy, and also on the more important scale of their success in operation. But in the balance must be put the conditions which preceded their adoption.

The crisis which the President entered was well described by the impartial and none too friendly Contemporary Review of London (George Glasgow) which in September 1935 said:

"Franklin Delano Roosevelt became President of the United States on March 4th, 1933. His period of office will therefore elapse in eighteen months' time from now. There is material enough to form a view of what he has attempted to achieve, and what he has achieved, in his historic Presidency; and he is in fact now being judged by the American electorate in preparation for the new election.

"The stage has even been reached where his personal character is being attacked, his integrity besmirched. That is absurd, but it is not more absurd than most of the tactics employed at most elections in most countries. No sane person ever doubted Mr. Roosevelt's personal integrity or the sincerity of his public purpose. He was put into office two and a half years ago by a scared United States.

"The machinery of civilized life in its economic and financial aspect had broken down. Money had ceased to function as a means of exchanging values. The banks had closed their doors against their panic-stricken creditors. The whole people of the United States were faced with the possibility of something like starvation merely because the confidence which enabled the daily necessities of life to be financed, organized and distributed, had been lost. A widespread feeling of helplessness forced Mr. Roosevelt willy-nilly into the position of an unquestioned despot. He was unanimously expected to do something, and to do it quickly, to restart the machinery that had stopped. He was left to his own absolute initiative and discretion to decide what to do.

"There are more than 100,000,000 people in the United States. Few men in history of the world have had thrust upon them a responsibility such as Mr. Roosevelt had to face. Yet he did something and did it at once. What he did, achieved its immediate object of enabling the 100,000,000 people to obtain the elementary necessities of life, and it re-established the confidence upon which money as a token of exchange in the buying and selling of goods and services could perform its function."

I submit that if Franklin Roosevelt had done nothing more than to keep the ship of state from foundering under the waves of disaster rushing upon it from every side, he would now be entitled to the support of his fellow citizens.

But he did much more. The ship saved, he busied himself in reconditioning it to ride out the storms of the future.

Let us examine his preparations.

2

A favorite attack upon the President's administration centers on the planning in which the New Deal is engaged. This criticism sometimes takes the form of condemning *all* attempts at social planning. Yet all governments, and practically every corporate body of size in modern society, seek constantly a program of planning. Surely the concept of planning for society is not to be struck down because in some instances the planning has miscarried. The proper contrast is not between planning and no planning, but rather between effective and ineffective planning.

An organized functioning society requires a planned economy. The more complex the society the greater the demand for planning. Otherwise there results a haphazard and inefficient method of social control, and in the absence of planning the law of the jungle prevails.

Sometimes the argument against the administration is based on the asserted tendency of the New Deal to regiment the population. The word "regimentation" has great popularity with critics, principally because it has a terrifying sound. But does any intelligent adult really feel that he has been "regimented"? Can he demonstrate that restrictions on his liberty are greater than when the Republicans ruled? After all, when two or more people live together the problems of restraint arise. The red traffic light is a form of regimentation typical of inevitable restraints of all stable governments.[1]

The essential distinction between the planning of the present administration and that of the previous one is that our present efforts are conscious and coherent and aimed at a definite goal. However we may label the present effort, the New Deal proclaims the view that if we are sincere in our desire to preserve democracy, we must attempt constructive measures to rehabilitate our economic and social methods. The point of the New Deal is that we do not need to have socialism with its accompanying disadvantages to do these things, but that an old political party, wise enough to comprehend the need of the day, can, within the framework of democracy, carry out by progressive legislation a comprehensive program of reconstruction.

[1] See Governor Alf M. Landon's address to Methodist District Conference, March 29, 1935, at Greeley, Colorado.

There is no doubt, therefore, that the New Deal has carried forward the concept of planning. This greater emphasis on planning resulted necessarily from the basic conditions which existed at the inception of the administration. In 1932, when the depression threatened ruin for everybody in the United States, when rapidly falling prices and tremendous corporate deficits were remorselessly crushing the country's economic life, sparing not bankers, nor industrialists, nor other persons of wealth, even the "rugged individualists" realized the merit of government action and of planned economy. The staggering losses of the depression clearly illustrated the need for greater planning. In 1929, we produced about 54,000,000 tons of steel ingots. In 1932, we produced only 13,000,000 tons of steel, a loss of over 40,000,000 unproduced tons. As a consequence, thousands of people who were directly or indirectly connected with the processes in the manufacture of steel were deprived of their jobs or were losing money. This experience was typical of all industries. The forgotten manufacturer, the forgotten industrialist, the forgotten financier, as well as the forgotten "little man" could each bear witness to the undermined faith and confidence of our nation. Their common plight called forth the necessity for future planning.

The depression awakened the social consciousness of all thinking people of the United States and created an overwhelming demand for a new social approach to economic problems. The administration of Mr. Hoover appeared blind to the necessity for this type of action, or unwilling to undertake it. Even the present critics of this administration are compelled to admit that "certainly a wiser business and political leadership could have done much to avoid some of the excessive manifestations of boom and collapse." It became increasingly clear to most people that the only way to control and avoid depressions was to regulate the "boom" periods preceding depressions, and that this required planning.

3

The overwhelming election of President Roosevelt, was an unequivocal expression by the people of the United States that they would not tolerate a political party unable or unwilling to grapple with the problem of planning. The people who voted for Mr. Roosevelt expected not only that action would be taken immediately to ameliorate their condition, but also that there would be evolved some cogent plan intended to give them a measure of future security. It was not just the unemployed who were of that mind. All competent bankers and industrialists who could avoid the spell of partisanship appreciated the need for planned action. Let me give you the record of a prominent banker's belief. In 1933, the late Mr. Otto H. Kahn said:

"(30 years ago) We believed that the benefit of the country required ruthless competition, however wasteful, and the devil take the hindmost. . . . We believed, in the pioneer period in the law of the jungle. . . . Now 30 years have come and gone since Mr. Theodore Roosevelt, and the 'new deal' is now being made. It is of the utmost consequence economically and socially. I do not believe any man is wise enough at this moment to express any views of conclusions until these new theories and laws have been tested. . . . May be that some of the matters which we have inherited from the past were wise after all and ought to be preserved. . . . I know a good deal must be changed. And I know the time is ripe to have it changed. Overripe in some ways."

The President described his philosophy of a planned economy during the 1932 campaign when he said:

"I have further described the spirit of my program as a 'new deal' which is plain English for the changed concept of the duty and responsibility of the government toward economic life . . . above all, my program has looked to the long view intending to see that the factors that brought about the present condition may not occur again."

It is not by any means contended here that the planning of the New Deal has been perfect. In its early stages, when the emergency was on us, hasty experimentation was necessary, with the inevitable reverses of policy, inconsistencies, collisions and mistakes. The impelling necessity for quick, vigorous and drastic action to relieve the nation from its dire predicament, of course, produced errors. But the administration was flexible, and able to correct itself, and all its efforts were sighted at a definite goal—to achieve, through the help of planning, greater stability and greater security in our economic life. The vital factor is that the Roosevelt administration realized the necessity for planning and that it had as a clear objective the rehabilitation and strengthening of our economy.

Its first and immediate objective, conquering the "depression," has been achieved. With respect to the long-term objective, the New Deal could not hope to reach that goal in the short period of three years. This reformation is a task for the years to come. We are faced now with the problem of weighing the accomplishments of the administration and analyzing the direction of its policies so that we may determine whether we wish to follow the path to a more stable economy as outlined by the President or to abandon the entire project and return to the Old Deal.

I shall attempt to present and analyze the major problems facing the government at the present time, to ascertain the approach of the New Deal towards these troublesome questions, to determine the methods of planning and the long-term outlook upon which such planning is based. Only thus can one evaluate the validity of much of the criticism now leveled at the administration.

Once again may I repeat, what should be a part of every politician's creed: that there is a sharp distinction between objective and method, and that dissatisfaction with a particular method should not obscure the objective. Unfortunately, current political discussion tends to relegate this simple incontrovertible truth.

CHAPTER III

In Which it is Contended that the New Deal is in the Black

THE administration is frequently attacked because of the size of the deficits and the increase in government debt during its tenure of office. One critic has phrased it: "The Hoover deficits, . . . totaled about $7,000,000,000 in four years. President Roosevelt's deficits in two years have totaled over $7,500,000,000." In seeking to analyze such figures, we must first endeavor to determine just how much the Roosevelt deficits have meant in terms of increased government debt.

From the end of February, 1933 to June 30, 1936, the net public debt of the United States excluding the increase in the balance on the general fund of the Treasury has increased about $10,400,000,000. In addition to this, the government has guaranteed bonds of Federal agencies so that contingent liabilities of about $4,700,000,000 have arisen during the period. But these figures alone exaggerate the increase. A correction should be made because some of the funds obtained through the sale of government bonds have been advanced to agencies which will eventually repay such advances. The most important of these is the Reconstruction Finance Corporation, a large portion of the assets of which are admittedly recoverable. The increase in the government's interest in such recoverable assets during the Roosevelt administration amounts to about $2,000,000,000 which should be balanced against the increase in debt.

The table on page 22 estimates the "real increase."

I have noticed the fact that four and three-quarters billion dollars of the debt increase represents contingent liabilities. These are guarantees of interest and principal of the Home Owners Loan Corporation and Federal Farm Mortgage Corporation bonds, secured by mortgages on urban and farm property. Perhaps there will be some losses on such property, requiring the government to make good on its guarantee. But a 20 per cent. loss ratio would seem very high and therefore certainly not more than $1,000,000,000 of the contingent liabilities should be regarded as an increase in debt.

A further adjustment in the debt increase should be made because the Stabilization Fund represents liquid and recoverable assets of the government. Consequently, the $2,000,000,000 in the Stabilization Fund should also be balanced against the increase in debt. If these adjustments are made, the increase, instead of being fifteen billion comes to about seven and a half billion dollars as is indicated in the table on page 22.

That the actual increase in government debt is much less than appears on first sight is, however, only one side of the picture. On the other hand there are the results, during the last three years, of the incurring of this debt. These deficits were the price

		($ billions)	
Net Government Debt:[1]			
February 28, 1933..........................	20.5		
June 30, 1936.............................	31.1		
Increase...............................		10.6	
From which there should be deducted the increase of the government's share in the recoverable assets of the Reconstruction Finance Corporation and other government corporations or credit agencies which are financed by appropriations from the Treasury			
Increase about.........................	2.0		
Also there should be deducted the assets of the Stabilization Fund which represent a cash resource of the Government			
Increase...............................	2.0		
Total............................		4.0	
These offsets which represent the gains in liquid assets by the Government, if deducted from the total increase in debt, make the real increase in the Government debt about..............		6.6	
To this should be added an amount estimated to cover the Government's possible loss as a result of the contingent liabilities because of its guarantee of Home Owners Loan Corporation and Federal Farm Mortgage bonds, both of which are well secured for the most part by conservative first mortgages. This possible loss on total contingent liabilities of 4.7 billion dollars and the government's capital investment in such agencies is estimated at not more than.................................		1.0	
Resulting in a total Real Increase in Debt from February 28, 1933 to June 30, 1936 of		7.6	

[1] After deduction of balance in General Fund.

paid by the people of the country to check a violent disruption of the existing order and peaceably to effect economic and social adjustment. The Roosevelt deficits were created in a vital attempt to breathe life into a nation apparently on the point of economic prostration.

The Hoover deficits, on the contrary, were not occasioned by expenditures made to revive a nation, and tended to strangle a people in the throes of what one critic has characterized as the "ultimate spasms of collapse."

2

The economic pathology of depressions is primarily the complete economic loss and deprivation to the nation of the labor of the unemployed. It is axiomatic and self-evident that the only economic cure for a depression is to put the people back to work. The forgotten man was not only the victim of the depression, but the lost man-power personified by the forgotten man was its basis and its measurement. Viewed from this platform, the economic cost of the depression (that is, the difference between national income produced in prosperous years and national income produced in the depression to date) is so large that the income lost would have enabled us to build anew the railroads, all public utilities, all our steel plants, all our mining and all other manufacturing industries as well. There are enormous resources to be tapped for financing a fully comprehensive program of recovery and rehabilitation. The funda-

mental approach of President Roosevelt to his problem was a concentrated application of the medication
of re-employment, putting the forgotten men on their
feet, thereby making it possible for them to become
profitable contributors to and beneficiaries of the
economic process. Expenditures for relief were thus
not the end in themselves but rather a means to
accomplish the desired end of putting people back to
work, both directly by creating jobs and indirectly
by increasing the demand for goods, thereby stimulating business and creating jobs. The money expended
served the dual function on the one hand of relieving
the distressing economic plight of a very substantial
portion of the population, and on the other of stimulating production.

Physically, the nation was ready for recovery, but
its financial system had collapsed, and the complex
economic organization of the United States is quite
dependent upon smooth operation of the system of
money and banking. The Hoover administration, and
many of the leaders of finance, simply did not realize
this fact, or if they did, lacked comprehension of a
method of restoration. Mr. Roosevelt and his Administration did understand, and did know what to do,
and how to do it. Success attended the effort with
remarkable promptness. The critics of the financial
policies and operations of the Administration should
take the time to compare their dire predictions with
the results.

The outlay necessary for the restoration of the
financial system can be measured in the loans and

advances to financial institutions, expenditures for insurance of bank deposits and savings and loan shares, the refinancing of homes under government auspices, and loans to railroads and other business institutions. Preponderantly funds used for all these purposes will be recovered, and so the cost will prove quite small.

Human needs were very great when the Administration took office, and the human resources of the nation had to be conserved. A relief program of many parts was undertaken. Socially this was imperative and economically it was necessary. Only the narrowest definition of economics excludes the individuals which make up the system. The basis of business is its customers.

The cost of relief, while not exactly measurable because relief expenditures served other purposes as well, totaled something like $6,000,000,000 during the three years. In terms of national income over the several years during which it can be paid, this cost is not very great. Viewed as an insurance premium on a large proportion of the population, the amount must be said to be reasonable. Or, from a different viewpoint, these expenditures are quite comparable to the large amounts business normally spends upon employee and customer welfare. Finally, this outlay had still other beneficial results, as shown in subsequent paragraphs.

For at the same time that the financial machinery was being restored, and welfare expenditures carried on, the normal and traditional methods of business recovery were being assisted by governmental financial operations. Deficit financing (together with gold imports) has sent demand deposits of banks, which comprise the preponderant part of money in the United States, to slightly above their 1929 levels. These deposits constitute the cash holdings of corporations and individuals. This rise in deposits, therefore, has financed rising business activity. In the past, this deposit rise has occurred as a result of business' borrowings from the banks, which borrowings are regarded as normal and economically healthful. As a result of such previous borrowings, business paid interest and amortized such loans to the banks.

Under the process which has occurred during the Roosevelt Administration, business will pay taxes to the government, and the Treasury will pay interest and principal to the banks. The essential results of the process are precisely the same in both cases: the borrowing is done, business gets the money to finance rising operations, and business profits provide for interest and repayment of the loans. Only the appearance of the present operation differs from that of preceding recoveries, not the actuality.

This process quite clearly applies to loans made by the government. But it equally applies to all deficit operations, for funds expended in any way, whether as loans or direct outlays, in the course of one or two expenditures, reach businesses, or individuals carrying on business. There is, therefore, a considerable offset to the relief expenditures, for they have in large part replaced the borrowing which business would have otherwise needed to do.

Business, as a result of this process, has not applied to the banks to any extent, despite the large rise in business volume. Bank loans have not risen with rising business. And an examination of the cash position of corporations is an explanation.

Another development which always occurs during business recoveries is the refinancing of debts at lower interest charges than those incurred during the preceding boom and depression. This process reduces the costs to business and individuals and increases their profits, thus assisting them in enlarging operations. This normal development the government has greatly assisted in two ways. First, large amounts of mortgage debt and some business debt have been refinanced under government auspices at lower rates of interest. Secondly, government operations have accentuated the reduction of interest rates in the money markets, and corporations have been able to carry through huge refinancing operations at a great saving to themselves.

3

A most striking fact about the whole debt situation, largely resulting from the operations above outlined, is one which the critics choose wholly to ignore. This is that the total debt in the country is now far lower than when the depression began. This is a fact which should normally be true during recovery periods, and is true during this one. Government debt has increased. But the long term debt of businesses and individuals is lower as a result of refinancing, reorganizations and repayments. And the short term debt of businesses and individuals is vastly lower. It should also be noted that the aggregate amount of state and city obligations is less than in 1933. All that has really happened is that the rise in the federal debt has only *partly* offset the decline in private debt of all kinds. So instead of owing each other in one form, we owe each other through the government. As a result of this process, we have been able to obtain an adequate amount of bank deposits although owing each other less in total. And we have been able to reduce the total interest charges as a result of having both a lower debt and lower interest rates.

The result of the three needed policies which the Administration has pursued—restarting the financial machinery, relieving the needy, and assisting recovery—has been prompt and excellent. Given the favorable conditions created by these Administration's actions, business promptly proceeded to revive, as the following facts show:

1. Industrial production in February 1933 was 64 per cent. of the 1923–25 average, having dropped during the depression from a maximum of 126 per cent. in May 1929. By May 1936 the index was 101, showing a recovery of 59 per cent. of the depression decline.

2. The index of factory employment as of February 1933 was 61 per cent. of the 1923–25 average, showing

a decline from 107 per cent. in August 1929. As of May 1936, the index was back to 86 per cent., having recovered 46 per cent. of the loss during the depression.

3. Factory payrolls were 40 per cent. in February 1933 as compared with 113 in September 1929, and were back to 79 per cent. in May 1936, having recovered about 55 per cent. of the drop.

4. The net income of all corporations filing income tax returns, which in 1932 was in the red in excess of $5,000,000,000 as compared with a profit of $9,000,000,000 in 1929, has shown a vigorous improvement. For 1935 this income is estimated at close to $2,000,000,000 in the black, or an increase of $7,000,000,000 from 1932. Present indications are that such net income may exceed $4,000,000,000 in 1936, indicating a recovery of almost two-thirds of the decline.

5. Automobile production in February 1933 was 105,000 passenger cars and trucks as compared with a high of 622,000 in April 1929. By May 1936 activity had increased to such an extent that production was 461,000, despite a shift in the seasonal peak back to November and December, so that almost 70 per cent. of the shrinkage of the depression has been made up.

6. Steel ingot production was 18 per cent. of capacity in January 1933 as compared with a high of 100 per cent. in June 1929, and had recovered to 71 per cent. in May 1936, or about 65 per cent. of the way back to 1929.

7. Building construction, after having dropped pre-

cipitously from a total of almost $6,600,000,000 in 1928 to only slightly over $1,000,000,000 in 1933, is approaching the $2,000,000,000 mark, with May 1936 almost as high as the equivalent 1931 figure, about a fifth of the drop thus having been recovered.

8. Carloadings in May 1933 aggregated 2,128,000 cars, having fallen from an average of 5,752,000 cars in 1929. They had recovered more than 26 per cent. of the loss by May 1936 when they totaled 2,679,000 cars (all figured on a four-week basis).

9. Prices of farm commodities, which in February and March 1933 stood at a low of 55 per cent. of the 1909–14 average as compared with a high of 152 per cent. in 1929, were back to 103 per cent. in May 1936, having recovered over 30 per cent. of the decline.

10. Cotton sold slightly over 5¢ a pound in June 1932 compared to a high of 21¢ in March 1929, and had recovered to about 12¢ in May 1936, or over 40 per cent. of the way back to 1929.

11. Wheat sold at 46¢ a bushel in December 1932 as compared with $1.30 in July 1929; in May 1936 it was 96¢, having recovered 60 per cent. of the decline from the 1929 level. A great deal of the improvement in agricultural prices is explained, by some, as due to the drought. That this has been but a minor and accidental cause, however, is best indicated by the fact that certain agricultural products which did not in any way suffer from the drought showed as much recovery from low prices as wheat. The increase in prices of these commodities, of course, was a result of a legis-

lative and administrative program and not the drought, and similarly for wheat and cotton. We had the AAA and other measures tending toward a systematized approach to the problem of agricultural prices, production and credit, and to these must go a great share of the credit for the improved farm situation.

12. Wholesale prices of all commodities as measured by the Bureau of Labor Statistics Index, which stood in February 1933 at 60 per cent. of the 1926 average as compared with a high of 96 per cent. in August 1929, rose in May 1936 to 79 per cent., a recovery of over 50 per cent. of the loss.

13. A minor increase has been shown by the cost of living index which in April 1933 was 72 per cent. of the 1923 average compared with 101 per cent. in October 1929 and rising in January 1936 to only 85 per cent.

This portrayal of improvement could be extended. Statistics of this sort, however, are difficult to view as a whole. It is better to approach the problem of the results of the deficits of the New Deal from a slightly different point of view: Assume that the whole increase in net government debt, including the contingent liabilities—i.e., the whole fifteen billion dollars, or roughly twice the real increase—has represented expenditures by the government in excess of its income for which borrowing has been necessary and against which no assets of any sort have been received. The increase in national debt on a per capita basis would then be about $120 with an annual interest cost of less than $3.00. If only the real increase in the net debt is taken into account the per capita increase amounts to about $60.

Borrowings by individuals from banks and an increase of such borrowings does not in and of itself necessarily call for condemnation. A study of the various factors motivating such borrowing is indispensable to the appraisal of their wisdom. If increased earnings result from borrowing, it is wholly justified. Similarly it is necessary to look at the profit and loss account of the Nation as a whole to ascertain whether this increased per capita obligation has been justified by an increase in earning power and wealth.

4

THE PROFIT AND LOSS ACCOUNT

The aggregate per capita national income at the inception of the Roosevelt administration probably did not exceed three billion dollars per month. For the year 1933, on the whole, it was slightly higher, but that income reflected many of the beneficial results of New Deal measures such as the NRA, the AAA, the revaluation of the dollar, etc. At the rate of three billion dollars a month the total annual income was thirty-six billion dollars which, apportioned among an approximate population of 125,000,000, amounted to $290 per capita. The national income today is estimated to be approximately five billion dollars a month or sixty billion dollars per annum.[1] This represents an increase of twenty-four billion dollars over the national income at the inception of the Roosevelt administration. The per capita increase is approximately $190 per annum. No individual would be criticized if, as a result of borrowing $120 at the cost of $3.00 per year, he succeeded in raising his salary $190 per year. On this basis, should we condemn or commend the administration?

Equally significant is the increase in national wealth. A fairly good barometer of the rise is the tremendous gain in the market value of stocks and bonds on the New York Stock Exchange. These securities are up approximately $42,000,000,000 from the lows of 1932. Not only were security prices in 1932 bottomless, but no real security market existed. Sporadic demands for the closing of security exchanges permeated the nation and finally culminated in the closing of exchanges with the banking holiday. Today, in addition to greater marketability for securities, we have increased prices. On the basis of this increase in New York Stock Exchange securities it can be estimated that all marketable securities in the United States, including those on all exchanges

[1] If present national income were adjusted to take account of the increase in cost of living since 1932, it would amount to about four and one-half billion dollars of 1932 purchasing power a month, an increase in real income of 50 per cent. However, the debt might also be adjusted in this manner, to express the burden in "real dollars," and on this basis the increase in debt would, of course, be substantially reduced.

and those on the over-the-counter market, have
increased approximately $100,000,000,000 from the
low of 1932–33, and even this increase does not include the rise in the value of the mortgages, farms
and other privately held property not represented by
marketable securities. This definitely conservative
estimate of $100,000,000,000, or about $800 per capita,
increase in national wealth alone is eight times the
maximum increase in the debt of the government.

Any business man who could borrow money and
put it to work so advantageously as to increase his
income, and thus the value of the outstanding securities of his corporation, would be judged very astute
indeed.

One need not be an astute financier or a profound
student of economics to appreciate the value of such
a course of conduct. Assume that the national debt
were increased by $25,000,000,000 instead of
$12,000,000,000, and the national income advanced
in the same proportion to the debt as heretofore
(assuming no greater change in the price level than
occurred from 1933 to 1936), the national income
would be up $50,000,000,000, exceeding the 1929
level. Would anybody seriously object? It might be
argued that limitations must be imposed on such
procedure if a runaway rise in prices is to be avoided.
This is conceded. However, a study of the ratio of
national debt to national wealth and income of some
of the outstanding foreign countries indicates that
our debt burden is still relatively low. The national
debt of the United Kingdom and of France is almost

200 per cent. of the annual national income in each country, while in the United States such debt is close to 50 per cent. of annual national income. If the debts of states and municipalities were included in the total, the ratio would be well above 200 per cent. in these two leading foreign countries as compared with perhaps 90 per cent. here. Measured in another fashion, our national debt is probably less than 20 per cent. of our national wealth, whereas the debt of the United Kingdom and of France is probably over 50 per cent. of the national wealth of those countries. On the basis of the experience of these countries, it would appear that mathematically, at least, we could increase our present debt more than two-fold in view of our national income and national wealth, without assuming a disproportionate burden.

The growth of debt to such a level is, of course, predicated on the assumption that our people will have the same patience and faith in those to whom they entrust the management of state affairs as the people of the older nations have had in their leaders. If our people lose faith in the government and the democratic process, then no matter how small in its ratio to income and wealth is the government debt, government credit will go. There will be a collapse. In other words, the prophets of disaster should concern themselves less with the size of the debt and more with the possibility that their insidious undermining of government authority, theoretically, at least, may bring about the very disasters they forecast.

The chance of this, fortunately, is very slim because, generally speaking, people who have an opportunity to witness monumental and favorable changes in their economic and financial conditions are ruled more by their sound instincts than by the half-thought-out philosophies of pseudo-economists who are convinced that our economic ills, like floods, and droughts, and earthquakes are beyond the control of man. Listening to these arguments, most of us are likely to wonder where we would be if we had followed this do-nothing idea, and so thinking are unlikely to lose confidence in a government which has formulated a constructive and intelligent program so long as this government continues to make strides towards recovery and towards the achievement of its program.

The true significance of the increase in national wealth and income which accompanies the increased national debt may be further clarified by a homely illustration. Assume that in 1932, President Roosevelt, acting for the nation, contracted with the numerous persons throughout the country who owned property which was on the verge of foreclosure, that, in consideration of his best efforts to rehabilitate their property and increase its value and the income derived therefrom, these owners would pay to the nation 10 per cent. of any such increase in value. By virtue of efforts of the administration, the people of the United States have benefited to the extent of $800 per capita. In accordance with his agreement each owner would now be required to turn over to the government, property to the value of $80. The government could either sell this property (and today real markets exist) and apply the proceeds in discharge of its indebtedness; or specifically apply this property in exchange for the outstanding evidence of the government's increased debt—its bonds.

If such an arrangement had been made, the result at the present time would be that all of the physical property, marketable and other wealth of the country would still be completely owned by the people of the United States, but would have an increased market value; while the real increase in government debt since President Roosevelt entered the White House ($5,000,000,000 plus estimated loss on contingent liabilities of $1,000,000,000) would be more than wiped out.

This is the recovery which has resulted from the positive contributions of the New Deal—reforms in banking, agriculture and industry, all aiming at a more balanced economy. In 1932 the theory that the improvement in the United States was delayed by unsettled international conditions was advanced as an excuse for Republican ineptitude. Perhaps they were right, but, whatever the cause, it is interesting to note that the domestic improvement above described has taken place in the face of an international situation which, in point of demoralization of currencies, tariff protection, political dangers, is probably the worst since the end of the World War.

5

Many speak critically of the President because of the vast burden of debt which he has piled up, "for our children to pay." Some who urge this criticism are sincere and well-meaning, happy at the thought of recovery, unhappy at the prospect of payment. Some, of course, are motivated by a resentment they feel for all social welfare measures, particularly those which appear costly. I submit that none of these critics have a proper appreciation of the nature of the debt and its relation to our whole economy, present and future.

Even if the spending policies of the Administration had resulted in a net increase in our indebtedness, the arguments applicable to the World War borrowing would suggest themselves immediately. The public debt arising from the Liberty Loan Drive was seldom questioned because the nation believed it was defending the firesides of generations yet unborn. That debt incidently was in large measure discharged by the generation which created it. The public debt of the Roosevelt Administration was incurred in waging a war which threatened the very foundations of our social structure more immediately and remorselessly than the World War.[2]

[2] The nature of the emergency and the measures to be followed were eloquently stated by Governor Landon himself in a speech February 12, 1933 for the Young Republican Club of Kansas City, Mo.

"I do not view the granting of extended powers to President Roosevelt as belonging in this class. I do not think it would endanger our democracy because, in the first place, we are at war. The effects of the last three years have been, and will be for a generation to come, as vital and drastic as those from any war in which this country has engaged. We cannot sit idly and let things drift. We have never felt it any confession of weakness inherent in a democracy to repose in our President the greatest power of any governmental head in time of war. To grant in a constitutional way all the power possible within the limits of our Constitution in time of peace—does not in my opinion endanger such government. The security of our present civilization is at stake."

However, we do not need to call to mind the war indebtedness to answer the present critics because their contention that the New Deal has placed a heavy and well-nigh unbearable debt on our children can be demonstrated to be fallacious.

In the first place, the total indebtedness in this country of all kinds is now less than when the New Deal began. In fact, our total indebtedness is less than that of 1929.

As will be developed more in detail the interest charges for our present debt have been greatly reduced. Through a scale-down in rural and urban mortgages, reductions in long-term obligations and financial and industrial companies, through re-organization (facilitated through bankruptcy laws of the administration), through recapitalization of several railroads, which, though not yet fully accomplished, are in process and are recognized by the markets, the aggregate of long-term indebtedness has been much diminished. Similarly, short-term debt has been noticeably cut down, largely by repayments which were made possible through increased profits resulting from the New Deal's activities. So, also, bank loans have been repaid at a rate clearly indicating the extent to which net debt reduction has taken place.

Because interest charges constitute the real burden of debt, the lowering of these charges is of tremendous importance in the general economy. Both long and short-term debts have been extensively refunded to a lower interest basis, a development which conservatively may be estimated to be within the range of 15 to 25 per cent. In view of the fact that the decline in other forms of debt has been greater than the rise in government debt, and in view of the reduced interest rates for all forms of indebtedness, it is nonsense to talk about the crushing debt burden. The obvious fact is that the debt has been shifted in form and somewhat reduced. Nor can it be said that we face an increased burden of taxation. The aggregate working capital position of this country is now greater than ever before in its history. Perhaps the greatest financial accomplishment of the New Deal has been this restoration of the nation's working capital from its state of near exhaustion in 1932.

The increase in government debt has occurred in such a way that bank deposits have been increased surprisingly. Had business borrowed from banks and from the capital markets to re-establish its cash and working capital position, it would have had to pay interest on the loans at a rate substantially higher than the government and would have had to amortize the debt. Governmental borrowing has replaced this direct borrowing and has functioned for the same purposes as private borrowing. Consequently, a considerable portion of the funds that business will pay as taxes would have had to be paid to private lenders as interest and amortization. As a matter of hard cold fact, business is substantially better off because the government did the borrowing, since the cost is less than business would have had to pay had it borrowed directly.

The idea that the existing government debt will require higher taxes than now exist, is unsound and manifests a misunderstanding of fiscal affairs. Existing tax rates operating upon existing national income (which, by the way, is likely to go higher) may be sufficient to balance the budget at the rate of expenditure of the last three fiscal years (excluding, of course, the bonus) and possibly also to provide funds for debt retirement.

It should be remembered that income taxes, which provide a very substantial portion of the government's revenue, reach the Treasury only after a considerable time-lag: those income taxes for the calender year 1936 will not begin to be paid in until the latter half of the fiscal year 1937, and the latter two installments will be paid in the fiscal year 1938. If, as is expected, there is increased prosperity and reduced expenditures, the accomplishment of debt reduction can be accelerated.

To any who may agree with this reasoning it is clear that the anxiety over "who will pay the debt?" is, to a large extent, a borrowed one. We have paid already by lending to the government, by paying taxes, and by undergoing a certain credit expansion. What counts is not the debt, but its relation to the underlying assets; to the income that is stimulated; to the purposes for which it was incurred; to the fashion in which it was incurred; and, what is more, to the total comprehensive program of recovery and constructive reforms which it has been financing. In such a comprehensive program deficits should tend to decline rapidly as business improves, disappear, and eventually be replaced by substantial sur-

pluses. The tax base will gradually widen and the
government debt contract.

With these considerations in mind, we can have
some idea of the *real* costs of the New Deal, com-
paring the deficits with their results. But, in addition
to these more definite factors, and the great economic
recovery, there has been an equally important recovery in the spirit of the country and the restoration
of confidence in our economic system. The forces of
despair, despondency and unrest have been repelled
and the fundamental institutions of our country
safeguarded. Thus, increasing debt has, because of its
accomplishments, brought not fear but confidence.
This fact is also indicated by the reaction of the
people of the United States and of the world at large
to government bonds. Our government credit is today
the highest it ever has been. The government is able to
borrow large sums of money at rates never before
known in the history of the country, and the annual
debt charges in 1936 will probably be less than
100,000,000 dollars higher than they were in 1933.
Despite the debt increase, the average cost of financing
has dropped from about 3.4 per cent. in February 1933
to about 2.6 per cent. in February 1936.

Measured on a per capita basis, the maximum increase in the carrying charges of the debt from February, 1933, to June, 1936, is about $1.00, or from
$5.50 to $6.50. In 1924, when the then outstanding
debt was approximately the same as in February, 1933,
when the New Deal started, the per capita carrying
charge was $7.75, or about *$1.25 more than at present*.

A critic of the New Deal writes:

"When you say a thing is effective you really mean two things:

"You mean it works . . . that it does what it is supposed to do, and—

"You mean that it gives you what is wanted without incurring a disproportionate sacrifice."

Measured by these standards, who can say that the increase in national debt has not been effective in accomplishing the purposes of reviving our economy?

Tables and charts are alarming exhibits for the casual or non-technical reader, I know. But those here presented (see appendix) fortify some of the foregoing arguments with hard facts, and make a bookkeeping account of the economic condition of the United States "before and after taking" the New Deal. They have been simplified in so far as it was possible without omitting essential details.

CHAPTER IV

In Which Unemployment Is Viewed on a Permanent Basis

I

A COMPARISON of our present economic position with our position in 1932 discloses that, although in many respects we are practically back to to the level of production of the more prosperous period in our history, there are still 10 to 12 million people unemployed. Moreover, it seems indisputable that if the government should suddenly and completely cease its relief activities, its public works program and allied measures, the number of unemployed would probably be increased considerably. The factors producing this situation are complicated and deeply embedded in the foundations of our economic structure, and the problem particularly emphasizes the need for planning, a fact which has been realized by the New Deal.

An analysis of the basic causes of unemployment discloses that this country, which normally saves about $10,000,000,000 per annum, measured in money income, saved only a small fraction of this amount in 1935. The small but positive savings in 1935, however, represent a remarkable recovery from a deficit in savings—i.e., a consumption of capital of far over $10,000,000,000 in 1932. Since the savings of the country are chiefly invested in so-called capital goods (plant equipment, buildings and other forms of durable producers' or consumers' goods), their low level has contributed to the relatively slow recovery in the capital goods industries. It is these industries, in many cases not yet operating profitably, which are responsible for large numbers of the unemployed. People who would normally be employed in the capital goods or allied industries, such as the railroads, have not all been receiving private pay envelopes to enable them to purchase consumers' goods, and thus keep the wheels of our economy in full motion. This factor aggravates the problem both directly and indirectly, through its effects on the manufacturers of consumers' goods. But, even in this field, the situation is tending gradually to improvement, although, in view of our changed requirements for capital goods and savings, it may take a long time to achieve complete readjustment.

A substantial cause of unemployment is the so-called technological displacement of labor. This problem is of such magnitude that it is not susceptible of solution overnight. The industrial efficiency, which is not undesirable, was accelerated the world over by the shortage of man-power created by the war, and by the necessity during the depression of keeping costs at a low level in order to avoid bankruptcy. Some experts contend that every economy in this direction, in the last analysis, means that some person is losing a job or that the raw material producer is receiving a ruinous price for his material. Theoretically, it seems obvious that, if we learn how to double the amount of output per unit of man-power, the thing to do is either to consume twice as much or to reduce our work time to one-half. But, after formulating this, we still do not know the solution. We do know that *longer* hours will not answer the problem; yet we seem today to be witnessing a gradual lengthening of the hours of work and a return to child labor (institutions which the NRA sought to abolish), so that the problem has, if anything, become more acute.

There is an additional problem arising from the normal growth in employables. These include a large group of people who sometimes reconcile themselves to a small income or to the charity of relatives, friends or organizations, but who in reality are employable, desire to work and therefore are really unemployed.

If we add those unemployed who lost their jobs because of the depressed state of the capital goods industries, those who have been displaced by machinery or by the reduction of foreign trade, those made surplusage by the increment in our working population occasioned by natural growth, and those who were idle even in the prosperous years, 1926–29, the 10,000,000 to 12,000,000 non-workers are accounted for.

Many of these are not new problems. However, 25 or 50 years ago, when we were still in a period of a rapidly expanding economy, when our geographic and our economic frontiers were still pushing forward, we were able to absorb easily the new man-power due to natural growth of population, immigration and improved industrial processes. Today, on the contrary, we begin with a heritage of accumulated unemployed resulting from the continuation of natural population growth (although immigration has virtually ceased), and from the cumulative effects of technological acceleration and dislocation of international trade. At the same time our economy has more or less become stable, or at least its rate of growth has been greatly reduced. These problems were not created by the New Deal. In fact, they were alleviated to the extent that the New Deal brought about recovery.

An excellent case study could be made of the British experience to demonstrate the point that our modern economy has been generating lack of employment which must be a permanent concern of governments. Business activity in England has for some months past exceeded the predepression peaks yet a substantial volume of unemployment still lasts there. This experience affords undeniable proof of the fact that unemployment is more than a depression phenomenon, that more than mere recovery at any cost to 1929 levels is needed.

Unemployment remains perhaps the most serious problem of the age. There is acute need for an intelligent industrial labor policy. The New Deal has attacked this difficulty on two broad fronts: relief for unemployed and long-range social security.

Relief per se is an unwelcome and undesirable method. People generally rebel against seeking charity. The administration of relief lends itself to abuses.

Abstractly, relief is economically wasteful, when there is not the automatic check of paying only for work or other value received. However, until a long-term policy of re-employment is formulated, there is no choice. We must take care of those victims of the dislocations of our economy, as best we can. Moreover, this is one case where good humanitarianism is good business, since helping these people has stimulated our national income.

Laying aside question-begging abstractions about "liberty" and the like, let us examine the problem which the President inherited. People just had to be fed—or else! I know of no higher duty or more noble function of the state than caring for the needy among our citizens. Pope Leo XIII, in his famous encyclical on the "Condition of the Working Classes," said,

"There is another and deeper consideration which must not be lost sight of. As regards the state, the interests of all, whether high or low, are equal. The poor are members of the national community equally with the rich; they are real component living members which constitute through the family the living body; and it need hardly be said that they are in every state largely in the majority. It would be irrational to neglect one portion of the citizens and favor another; and therefore public administrators must duly and solicitously provide for the welfare and comfort of the working classes. Otherwise that law of justice will be violated which ordains that each man shall have his due."

This principle of government meant that under the circumstances large sums of money had to be ex-

The government is attempting to make its projects useful and valuable even though these projects may not always involve construction. The essential thing to remember is that we are securing the effect of the dole in caring for the physical needs of those on relief, plus other advantages. As already indicated, the only way to reduce the real loss, that is, the real cost of a depression, is to cut down the idle economic energy of the beneficiaries of relief by converting it into useful projects. It is true that because of the pressure of time and our depression unpreparedness, inherited from previous administrations, it was difcult to do much along such lines at the begi

This method of attacking unemployment cized as expensive and uneconomic. Ba ever, it is the soundest method, becau continuous and permanent addi resulting from public works the theory that they are demoralizing effect of and destroying th economic cheapnes established. A usefu on our wealth and well Tri-borough Bridge is a spent on such projects, pa brings about several turns resulting in two or three dollar lating the entire economy in seve the dollar of dole money circulates a the banker and the candlestick mak

---

pended. It meant that our national budget had to be out of balance. Critics who call for a balanced budget in a time of such great stress are seeking the impossible. There is no large group in this country which would desire a balanced budget if it necessitated a denial of that form of government aid to which the group has become accustomed. The testimony of the non-government experts who appeared before the Senate Committee on Finance and the general viewpoint of economic experts show how baseless is our panic about deficits. A new tax bill, and the intelligent tax program and the relief bills easily will be paid.

2

The little opposition which once was directed against relief for the needy has disappeared. The debate is addressed to the allocation of the responsibility between State and Nation and locality and State. Lately there has been a suggestion that we have all relief on a charitable basis—a sort of national Community Chest. Such talk is foolish. Any man of sense can support a relief program which is complete and fair to the needy is social insurance. Perhaps the premium is high but the property to be protected is so vast as to defy valuation. We have had numerous instances to show how ugly and menacing hungry men may become. Apart from that it is unthinkable that responsible persons should seriously advocate that the care of the needy is not a problem of the State.

Caring for the indigent on a purely business basis.

Until we are ready with definite plans for redistributing work, whereby we can employ all the people capable of doing work, our best hope lies in stimulating production, increasing national income and getting more people off the relief rolls, thus lightening the burden of financing relief. During this period, increased tax returns may be necessary. These taxes will represent, to the extent that their proceeds are applied to relief, a part of the economic product of the employed transferred, with the help of the government, to those unable to find employment. It is quite possible that for several years to come at least a portion of the present unemployment will remain a permanent part of our economy, a condition which existed before the 1929 collapse.

... European countries even before the 1929 collapse.

Hence provision for such expenditures may have ... be made in our budget.

How should the government spend mon... lief? When money is supplied on the b... goods, but one side of the norma... the recipients spend the fund... lacking. The government has... do its relief job in wha... barreled manner, whi... way of attacking... making an eff... only to alle... only to... nee...

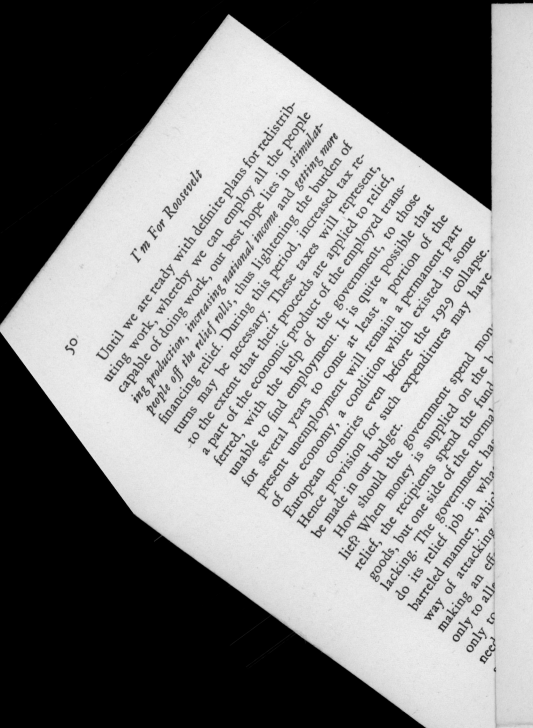

for public works circulates, in addition, among producers of the raw materials and finished building materials, the transportation agencies, etc. With each such expenditure some person is put to work, stimulating the economic body, spreading confidence, energizing the whole economic process.

While no careful studies of the subject have been made, it has been estimated that for every one man that finds employment in public works, at least one additional man, and according to some estimates, perhaps two more, find employment, some supplying the materials, others supplying goods for construction, and others supplying services, consumers' and capital goods (houses, motors, etc.) to those who receive money for their raw materials and labor. The chain has many links.

The New Deal has also proceeded on the theory that Federal direction is necessary for these relief projects. It is not difficult to recall the obstacles which states and cities had to overcome in coping with their unemployment problems. After organized campaigns, led by the outstanding financial and business leaders, New York City in 1931 and 1932 managed to raise just enough money to give the unemployed of the city, if all of them had been cared for, sustenance for perhaps a few weeks. Therefore, to say that these essentially national economic problems can be handled on a state or city basis is nonsense. The problem is national in scope because of the inability of the states to finance. And the need is widespread and cannot be handled purely on a local basis. If there were some progressive states anxious to initi-

pended. It meant that our national budget had to be out of balance. Critics who call for a balanced budget in a time of such great stress are seeking the impossible. There is no large group in this country which would desire a balanced budget if it necessitated a denial of that form of government aid to which the group has become accustomed. The testimony of the non-government experts who appeared before the Senate Committee on Finance which was considering a new tax bill, and the general viewpoint of economic experts show how baseless is our panic about deficits. A few years of prosperity with an intelligent tax program and the relief bills easily will be paid.

2

The little opposition which once was directed against relief for the needy has disappeared. The debate is addressed to the allocation of the responsibility between State and Nation and locality and State. Lately there has been a suggestion that we have all relief on a charitable basis—a sort of national Community Chest. Such talk is foolish. Any man of sense can support a relief program which is complete and fair to the indigent on a purely business basis. Caring for the needy is social insurance. Perhaps the premium is high but the property to be protected is so vast as to defy valuation. We have had numerous instances to show how ugly and menacing hungry men may become. Apart from that it is unthinkable that responsible persons should seriously advocate that the care of the needy is not a problem of the State.

Until we are ready with definite plans for redistributing work, whereby we can employ all the people capable of doing work, our best hope lies in *stimulating production, increasing national income* and *getting more people off the relief rolls*, thus lightening the burden of financing relief. During this period, increased tax returns may be necessary. These taxes will represent, to the extent that their proceeds are applied to relief, a part of the economic product of the employed transferred, with the help of the government, to those unable to find employment. It is quite possible that for several years to come at least a portion of the present unemployment will remain a permanent part of our economy, a condition which existed in some European countries even before the 1929 collapse. Hence provision for such expenditures may have to be made in our budget.

How should the government spend money for relief? When money is supplied on the basis of direct relief, the recipients spend the funds for consumers' goods, but one side of the normal economic process is lacking. The government has therefore attempted to do its relief job in what may be called a double-barreled manner, which is economically the soundest way of attacking the problem. The government is making an effort in its public works projects, not only to alleviate the suffering of the unemployed, not only to secure the desirable effect of supplying the needy with money whereby they can purchase consumers' goods, but also to link up the establishment of such purchasing power with the creation of lasting wealth.

The government is attempting to make its projects useful and valuable even though these projects may not always involve construction. The essential thing to remember is that we are securing the effect of the dole in caring for the physical needs of those on relief, plus other advantages. As already indicated, the only way to reduce the real loss, that is, the real cost of a depression, is to cut down the idle economic energy of the beneficiaries of relief by converting it into useful projects. It is true that because of the pressure of time and our depression unpreparedness, inherited from previous administrations, it was difficult to do much along such lines at the beginning.

This method of attacking unemployment is criticized as expensive and uneconomic. Basically, however, it is the soundest method, because of the obvious continuous and permanent additions to our wealth, resulting from public works. Doles are advocated on the theory that they are "cheaper." Aside from the demoralizing effect of the dole, in encouraging loafing and destroying the moral fiber of the recipient, the economic cheapness of this method has never been established. A useful project leaves permanent traces on our wealth and well-being. New York City's great Tri-borough Bridge is an illustration. One dollar spent on such projects, particularly on public works, brings about several turns of the economic wheel, resulting in two or three dollars of income and stimulating the entire economy in several directions. Just as the dollar of dole money circulates among the butcher, the banker and the candlestick maker, so the dollar

for public works circulates, in addition, among producers of the raw materials and finished building
materials, the transportation agencies, etc. With each
such expenditure some person is put to work, stimulating the economic body, spreading confidence,
energizing the whole economic process.

While no careful studies of the subject have been
made, it has been estimated that for every one man
that finds employment in public works, at least one
additional man, and according to some estimates,
perhaps two more, find employment, some supplying
the materials, others supplying goods for construction, and others supplying services, consumers' and
capital goods (houses, motors, etc.) to those who receive money for their raw materials and labor. The
chain has many links.

The New Deal has also proceeded on the theory
that Federal direction is necessary for these relief
projects. It is not difficult to recall the obstacles
which states and cities had to overcome in coping
with their unemployment problems. After organized
campaigns, led by the outstanding financial and
business leaders, New York City in 1931 and 1932
managed to raise just enough money to give the unemployed of the city, if all of them had been cared
for, sustenance for perhaps a few weeks. Therefore,
to say that these essentially national economic problems can be handled on a state or city basis is nonsense. The problem is national in scope because of the
inability of the states to finance. And the need is widespread and cannot be handled purely on a local basis.
If there were some progressive states anxious to initi-

ate sound programs, they would find themselves faced with migration from less progressive states. The problem is essentially a national one.

The steel workers in Gary are working for a national market. The depression in the steel industry is no more an Indiana problem than it is a New York problem. Furthermore, it is more than a problem of one industry; not alone steel, but agriculture, transportation, construction, and every other phase of our national economy is affected. The state approach to such problems is inept. Of course state or even local administration may be more efficient and hence decentralization may be desirable. But that is something else again, quite different from classifying the problem as local.

3

These observations do not deal with the long-run solution of unemployment. That is tied up with the question of social security and general industrial planning towards which this administration has undoubtedly made some progress. Eventually, perhaps, we may be able to achieve the regularization of employment which is the only logical attack upon our problems. Today, we pay a carpenter $10 a day, but if he works only 100 days during the year, his salary is only $1,000. Because carpentry work is expensive, we say we cannot employ him more regularly. As a necessary corollary, if a carpenter is to survive at all, he has to receive higher compensation for the days he is working.

This vicious circle has to be broken somehow. The

nation cannot exist without receiving important services, because these services are expensive, while the working men who do not get enough work are thus forced to ask almost prohibitive wages for the days they work. Since the carpenter is interested in his yearly income, eventually we may be able to attack this problem by stabilizing employment throughout the year from 100 days to 250 days at, say, $6 a day. The carpenter would then make $1,500 a year or 50 per cent. more than at the present. The nation would get much more carpentry work done than at present, since prices would be lower and people would be willing to spend more.

The result would be that we would spend $1,500 a year instead of $1,000 for carpentry work and would get 250 days work instead of 100 days. The amount of carpentry would be $2\frac{1}{2}$ times as much as at present. The national wealth by such a system would be increased and from that fact would flow additional advantages to all classes.

Because this problem is tied up with so many phases of our national economy, and is a symptom of maladjustment within this economy, it must be dealt with in conjunction with a general national plan. Such a plan must draw upon the resources of all fronts of our economy, including industry itself, which thus far has not shown either much cooperation or particularly sound judgment. If industry were really anxious to help in solving this problem, it could have taken forward steps under the NRA. It could have attempted to reduce overhead by expanding output, thus reducing prices and taking full advantage of latest consumer demand. Instead, in many cases, prices were raised, and in effect there was formed a conspiracy against the consumer, who, in his position as a final arbiter in the economic process, limited his purchases.

To whom shall we entrust the task of coping with this problem? Shall we entrust it to the Old Dealers who did not recognize the existence of these basic factors? Shall we entrust the task to those former Old Dealers who have, in some ways, adjusted their ideas and possibly now recognize the existence of the crucial question? Unfortunately, even they would prefer to rely on free competition and an absence of every form of regulation which of necessity tends toward monopoly, since they have no real urge to make an effort, now that they themselves have been saved.

Whatever we may think politically, the problem of unemployment and relief is a present, vital one and we shall be more, not less, conscious of it in the years ahead. I am for the man who had the wisdom to see it and the courage to meet it. One of the President's methods (the NRA) was declared invalid, but such declarations never solved anything.

CHAPTER V

In Which the Causes and Consequences of Devaluation are Listed

THE significance of our foreign trade situation with reference to unemployment has been mentioned. Our foreign trade at least in its post-war phase was, to a large extent, dependent upon our foreign loans. With the cessation of loans as retaliation for the poor record of debt repayment we cannot expect any expansion in our exports except to the extent that we increase our purchases from abroad. With our own plants only partly employed, we cannot buy large quantities from foreign countries, and therefore only a small increase in foreign trade is possible.

In addition to the barriers of financing, the whole question is complicated by the unsatisfactory general international situation which has become more aggravated during the last two or three years. There appears little hope, therefore, for improvement in the near future in view of the almost universal tendency to raise tariffs and to create other artificial barriers to the international exchange of goods.

Several million people in the United States were directly or indirectly dependent for profitable employment upon export and import trade. The present state of that trade is therefore an important element in our as yet unsettled economic situation. The activities of the State Department taken in the direction of Reciprocal Trade Agreements, although they are in their infancy, indicate a recognition of the underlying ill and the sound cure. Any basic solution must await improvement in the general international situation.

One phase of this question has been the stabilization of currencies. A frequent reproach against the administration relates to its monetary policy. The fact that President Roosevelt has cleaned up the sick banking situation which existed in 1933 is rarely mentioned. It is now forgotten by some that as recently as 1933 the great majority of depositors were fearful about the loss of their deposits. Many of them experienced the tragedy of losing their jobs and then returning home to find their savings lost in the débris of a bank failure.

As a part of planning towards a stronger banking structure the government adopted the principle of insured deposits. The financial community, and the large banks in particular, in accordance with custom, bitterly opposed such insurance. This viewpoint, however, has changed, and it is generally admitted that our banking structure is much stronger today because of this insurance feature.

But what of the promise of "a sound currency to be preserved at all hazards," as contrasted with the President's devaluation of the dollar and his stopping conversion into gold?

The devaluation of the dollar, actually promulgated by President Roosevelt, merely reflected a condition he inherited. The event was an inevitable result

of the policy of the previous administration which
forced us off the gold standard. Early in 1933 the New
York bankers themselves clamored for a holiday,
despite "the sanctity of a promise" and despite their
solemn obligations to their depositors.

On the night of March 3, 1933, the Committee of
the Clearing House banks of New York City requested
the Governor to proclaim a bank holiday. These
words were, in part: "The request of the Clearing
House Committee to the Governor is based on the continued and increasing withdrawals of currency and
gold from the banks of the country. The unthinking
attempt of the people to convert over forty billion
dollars of deposits into currency at one time is on its
face impossible."

The instinct of self-preservation manifested itself
and the existence of a "force majeure" justified their
steps. They desired a state sponsored banking holiday
because there was no other alternative. It was holiday
or receivership. The tremendous hoarding had to be
stopped if we were still to enjoy a banking system.
The gold had to be preserved if we were to have gold
reserves for the money remaining in this country. The
New York Reserve Bank was losing gold at a rate
which, if continued for an additional week or so,
would have meant loss of all our gold.

These are the historic and undisputed facts. The
administration's steps did not involve any repudia-
tion.

In the 1932 campaign, President Hoover said we
were, at one time in 1931, on the verge of going off the

gold standard. Whatever the facts were, there undoubtedly was some basis for the statement. And later the evidence of bank failures and state holidays showed the unsoundness of the financial structure which Mr. Roosevelt inherited. Because of these conditions in March, 1933 and earlier, it is clear that the devaluation was a result of events prior to the New Deal.

While the necessary degree of devaluation was not easily determinable, it was obvious that the only quick and sure way to dilute the debt to reduce its crushing weight, or rather to bring it back nearer where it stood in 1926, whence it had risen solely because of the tremendous fall in prices, and to stop the spiral of deflation which was the fundamental cause of hoarding, was to make the dollar a little less valuable and commodities and services a little more valuable. That could only be accomplished by going off gold first and revaluing the dollar afterwards. The devaluation of the dollar was thus merely the superficial expression of the deflation forces of the period, 1929–32.

However, the causes for this deflation went back to the span from 1925 to 1929. Devaluation was born during the Hoover years but conceived during the "Coolidge prosperity." Stabilization came with Roosevelt, the reflection of a confident feeling that the mildly expansive policy of the New Deal would allow a return to a stable dollar. As a result, the United States currency today, as everybody knows, is one of the strongest currencies in the world. To have attained this position, after the threat of a complete loss of our gold as a result of bank runs by depositors, solemnly attests the sound economics and financial leadership of the President.

He succeeded where professors of economics failed, because he had an unprejudiced mind, whereas they were serene in their knowledge of a theory based on a narrow philosophy suitable only to the early expansive stage of our economic career. These theories attained orthodoxy in the minds of some, because they coincided with the interests of a small moneyed aristocracy, and to this group such theories had the sanction of immutable laws. Such economic thinking was very likely sound in the Colonial and Post-Colonial years. In those times, a growing credit economy (that is, a debt economy), could be supported by rapid accumulation of capital and a great out-pouring of goods, i.e. a rapidly expanding economy. Then we were in what might be called the Exploitation Stage. But to continue the rate of growth of a debt structure when we have reached a more sedate period, when capital accumulation and output are slowing down, a time when we are in what might be termed the Management or Conservation Stage, would appear to be unsound.

With respect to stabilization, the President has refused to permit himself to be stampeded into hasty international action in currency matters at a time when the entire world is undergoing serious revisions of currency thoughts. Subsequent events proved once more the soundness of the President's judgment in refusing to be precipitated prematurely towards stabilization in the London conference, and these events have also indicated the unsoundness of some of his impatient critics.

The problem of stabilization cannot be singled out of the context of other New Deal problems. Stabilization is not the end. It is not an aim, but a means to strengthen our whole economic and social structure and to assist in the fixture of world economics. Regulation with respect to currency must thus be viewed, not as a thing apart but as one component of the broader purposes of the administration.

From this viewpoint, currency and budget health, supervised by a carefully planned system, with definite objectives and definite means to achieve them, can be protected from any real threat, when such a threat appears. Despite partisan talk about "boloney dollars," the dollar bill in your pocket, Mr. Citizen, is every bit as good as, if not better than, the dollar of the nineteen twenties.

CHAPTER VI

In Which the Farm Problem is Reviewed

I

THE agriculture program of the administration (and I venture to discuss it because it lies distinctly in the economic field) has been criticized on the basis that there is no real difference between the old Farm Board (attacked in the Democratic platform of 1932) and the AAA. The farmer, who is not a quibbler, must appreciate the difference: under one system he was becoming more and more impoverished; under the other he has been perceptibly recovering his economic wellbeing.

What is the difference between the Farm Board and the AAA?

Both the President and the Democratic Party condemned the Farm Board on the ground that the agricultural problem could not be solved merely by buying wheat, without restricting the forces of production. If, in addition, there is a promiscuous bounty of seed loans and new land opened by irrigation, it is clear that production will increase, while the high prices caused by Government purchases will tend to reduce consumption.

The New Deal approach to agricultural rehabilitation is through a different avenue. It aimed primarily to control the output in order to increase the farmer's total income. Orations and appeals to the farmers to desist from planting and to cooperate are not a substitute for an agricultural policy and can never be effective, because every farmer naturally thinks in terms of his own farm and is not certain the other farmers will cooperate with him. A program (call it subsidies, if you please) financed by the processing taxes was necessary to make such effective control possible.

The New Deal never claimed that the AAA was the complete agricultural policy. It was seeking light in several different directions, and, during the progress of the AAA, it recognized the acuteness of the sharecroppers' plight and other complications. The AAA, however, outlined a program which was necessary under the emergency to bring about better prices for the farmer. Without such prices, any policy would have been thwarted. Unless large excess outputs could be exported (and the international situation made it impossible for us to export) it was impossible to maintain fair prices for increasing production.

Inability to maintain fair prices for agricultural products is reflected in inability to maintain a structure of fair prices and adequate volume for all industries. If the farmers are "broke," the insurance companies and the banks are affected, the factories are unable to employ industrial workers, and, all along the economic structure there are stresses and strains.

The inducements to farmers, therefore, to control production were conceived for the benefit of our whole economy. The basic idea is that you can maintain a certain price level in any commodity only if you have a definite limited supply. This idea stems from economic laws that lend themselves to definite measurements of prices in relation to supply.

A reasonable and decent price was desired, and yet a price which would permit consumers to satisfy their normal requirements and habits. Therefore, the price relationships before the War were chosen as normal. Certainly prices have risen as a result of this program —perhaps $\frac{1}{2}$¢ on a loaf of bread. But is it not better to buy at that increased price than, with bread selling for 2¢ less, be able to get it only by/in the bread lines?

Processing taxes and subsidies were designed for the purpose of keeping the output at the desired level and maintaining prices that would allow an output within the absorptive capacity of the market, and thus insure an economic price to the farmer and a normal functioning of our production, exchange, and credit machinery in general.

2

It has always been considered good business judgment in industry to limit production to the extent that the market can absorb the product. This is called the talent of management. It would be suicidal for an automobile manufacturer, for example, to go on producing without limit. An executive who followed such a policy would soon be removed from his position, either by the stockholders or by the insolvency of the company. The agricultural problem is more difficult than any of our industrial questions because for generations our agriculture was developed to service world markets, a large part of which suddenly disappeared in 1931.

The average man may not have a clear understanding of this difficulty, but the farmers appreciate the problem. The farmers are well aware also of the pious generalities of the Republican spokesmen. President Roosevelt was the first leader to wrestle with the problem realistically and not evade it with platitudes.

The Republicans are now once more wooing the farmer. But this time they must woo with a ring. People who are familiar with financial markets, securities and commodities, know that excessive crops result in low, ruinous prices (when they speculate they sell such crops short), just as a short crop results in high prices (when they speculate they buy such crops for a rise).

Everybody realizes that a better way to solve the question of surpluses is to increase consumption, and this is the direction in which the New Deal is looking for its eventual solution. However, since nobody has been able to suggest a practical method of accomplishing this result quickly, the only remaining device is to reduce production to the level of reasonable demand and then gradually try to increase both production and consumption.

The experience of the Farm Board indicated that just such action was necessary if we were to avoid a collapse. Without such steps, the loss would have encompassed everything and all values would have disappeared.

In general, the argument against the AAA and the agricultural policy which accuses the New Deal of following a plan of scarcity, cannot hold water. The very aim of the New Deal is the opposite; that is, the achievement of greater abundance for the people; but it is recognized that to reach this goal not only is greater production required, but also a method for distributing the product is necessary. In the light of this fact, and other considerations, the agricultural policies of the administration are logical, necessary, and part of a rounded plan for the achievement, not of scarcity, but of abundance and its permanency.

Unrestricted production does not mean greater distribution of farm products among all the people of the United States. On the contrary, unrestricted production leads to low prices which limit distribution. In the recent past we observed over-production causing low prices, which, in turn, restricted shipments of farm products, because the price of the commodity, in many cases, would not have paid the costs of shipping it. We saw corn used as fuel and other food stuffs permitted to rot on the ground. Eventually, too, the economic repercussions are such that industrial wage-earners remain idle and have no money to buy even at low prices. There is, thus, abundance that results not only in scarcity, but also in waste, on the one hand; and in hunger on the other. Furthermore, low prices, if they continue for a long enough period, force the farmers drastically to cut production below the minimum requirements of the nation. These are types of abundance that produce a real, and not an apparent scarcity.

A planned effort to control production achieves, in the long run, the very opposite of scarcity. But under a laissez faire system scarcities develop as the result of low prices which do not reimburse the farmers for their time and out-of-pocket expenses, and thus restrict production. Scarcity also results where low prices do not cover transportation costs, and is intensified when a continued era of such prices physically weakens the producers of commodities so that they cannot go on raising and harvesting crops. But there are other and worse kinds of scarcities that may develop, and actually did develop in 1933 as a result of the limited laissez faire abundance.

What was the prologue to the AAA? There was more than this simple and passive limitation of the distribution of farm products. There were, also, the more explosive and violent methods of the farm holiday, arising out of the disgust, disappointment and despondency of ordinary humans who saw no satisfactory returns from their labor. There was, thus, a threat of the worst kind of scarcity—that which comes from mob action and revolution.

These are the reasons why the AAA and its limitations on production appear to have been necessary as a method of raising prices, and as part of a plan leading to a greater and a lasting abundance.

Our agricultural policy, offered to meet an emergency, is not finished or perfect. It necessarily could not be for two vital reasons:

First, the pressure of emergencies and our inherited unpreparedness to cope with them. The Old Dealers had made no effort to study either the fundamental causes of the agricultural difficulties or the bases for rehabilitating an agricultural economy, built on world markets, which had to readjust itself to a domestic basis once we stopped lending to foreign countries. Up to the very brink of the debacle President Hoover saw the solution only in terms of loans to foreigners. In the light of foreign defaults this was equivalent to a policy of gifts.

Second, the New Deal is still in its formative period, and the agricultural problem, like many others, is too complex to be susceptible of ready solution by any simple formula. Years of study, planning, and experimentation are required, and the New Deal, with consciousness of the necessity for study and willingness to do so, is confident it can cope with the situation. Its confidence is based on the success of its first attack on the emergency existing in agriculture. The facts that, in these early stages, imperfections crept in and that some of the policies represented compromises with unenlightened interests are not so important and certainly do not create an unsurmountable obstacle toward the goal.

What is important is the direction in which the New Deal has travelled. That the New Deal has vigorously attacked this problem and has already improved farm prices considerably must be conceded by even the most bitter critic of the Administration. If the present efforts of the government are abandoned, we shall have to start all over again with this basic problem of agriculture and all the experience of the New Deal will be wasted.

But why should we repudiate the New Deal's efforts to improve agriculture and substitute the Republican platform? Who would be better off? Not the farmer, not the working man whose prosperity is linked with the farmer's, not the business man. The speculator might gain, but shall we adjust our policies for his benefit? In agriculture, as in many other spheres, in order gradually to attain a finished product in point of a constructive scheme of permanent rehabilitation, there must be afforded the opportunity which time gives to continue the job started along those lines which have already proved measurably successful.

Who stands forth in opposition to the President with a clear-cut condemnation of the Administration's farm program and a courageous and intelligent counter solution? No one. The Administration is given a reluctant blessing or the farmers are offered the basic plan in other words by those who previously were not able to devise a plan to aid them.

CHAPTER VII

In Which the Relation of Taxes to the New Deal Program is Set Out

I

AMONG the more violent criticisms against the the New Deal are these: it is too costly; its taxes are too heavy; it is ruining the government's credit. These illustrate the type of critical barrage which a government of action, made necessary by conditions it inherited, must face. If one were to be persuaded by all the critics, each doctor with his own pet panacea, the government should not have raised taxes, should not have borrowed from the banks, or from investors, should not have attempted any changes in the currency. In fact, if all these had been followed, the government would long ago have stopped functioning and the patient (our national economy) would have been buried for three years.

Chapter III was an attempt to show that the New Deal has not been costly in the light of its accomplishments. It leads properly to a consideration of the wisdom of methods of financing and raising revenue.

Some critics of the President say he should have financed the New Deal chiefly by taxation, others that he should have taxed less and borrowed more, and still others that he should have paid for the relief and other agencies by expanding currency.

The President has followed the only sound approach

and employed all three methods. Suppose the President completely relied upon one method to the exclusion of others.

a. Heavy taxation: To resort to this exclusively during a depression is to gamble that the national income will not be reduced and thus contract the taxable field. With a reduction in national income, tax returns actually decline in spite of increased rates and bases of taxation. With a decline of income and revenues the government problems of unemployment and relief become more acute as its income drops. To have relied wholly on taxation would have killed enterprise and production. A weak body cannot generate energy, and to saddle the sources of revenue with additional burdens at a time of poor business is to weaken them further.

Eventually, as prosperity returns, the whole basis of our taxation should be revised, with a tendency for taxation to expand vertically (tax rates) and horizontally (number of tax-payers) with a contraction of both if depression reoccurs. If people are to continue to work and industry is to be stimulated, thereby reducing the number of victims of the depression, taxation should be expanded gradually.

b. Excessive borrowings: To follow exclusively a course of borrowing by the government, to draw upon the accumulated savings of our people, with a view to paying these debts when conditions improve, is to gamble upon the impairment of the government credit and increase the cost of carrying the debt. If, during the depression, when confidence and savings are at a low ebb, people are reluctant to buy government bonds, and interest rates increase, the whole structure of values of securities is jeopardized. The increased purchasing power given to people on relief is offset by the reduction in ability-to-purchase of those who spend their savings to buy government bonds. The method then acts as a damper on business improvement, and thus defeats its very purpose. The avenue of borrowing has to be gradually expanded, and as prosperity returns the government debt should be shifted to a greater number of people.

c. Excessive expansion of credit: To follow exclusively a policy of expansion of credit is dangerous in that a debauch of currency and a run-away inflation may ensue, as happened in Germany after the World War. A moderate stimulation of the price level as a result of credit expansion is, of course, desirable to bring back past relationships of prices and remunerations. But an extreme use of that means would bring collapse and, by a tragic dénouement, aggravate a depression by robbing the people of their savings in the form of bank deposits, bonds, mortgages, insurance policies, etc. Just as the other means have to be expanded when business conditions improve, so credit should be carefully controlled and its expansion definitely stopped once we are in higher altitudes of prosperity. (The New Deal devised machinery to control this phenomenon, and the Federal Reserve Board employed it in July 1936.)

2

What actually happened? These were precisely the three means used to finance rehabilitation but they were used in combination. The exact dose given of each is difficult to fix, nor is it known what the proper dosage should be. But the medication was handled in such a way that the extreme consequences of any of those methods have been avoided. The extreme consequences of the taxation method (seizure of all property or capital levy on confiscatory rates), of the expanding of credit (a run-away inflation), and of excessive borrowing (a grave impairment to the government credit and the purchasing power of the people), were averted, while we financed a winning war against the depression. It would, therefore, appear that the various present methods of financing the New Deal have been the least painful and probably the most constructive, even though, as prosperity returns, there may be considerable change required in our technique of raising government revenue.

The taxation problem is very complex and the taxation policy of the New Deal like any other policy, is far from being a perfect and finished product. There are, however, certain definite plans which the President has in mind in coping with the problem. By trying to follow the principle of ability to pay, he has endeavored gradually to improve our taxation system. What is frequently forgotten in criticizing methods is that the ability of making money is only to a degree dependent on the talent of the maker. It is, to a much larger extent, dependent upon the context of economic and social conditions which make it possible for the money-maker to utilize the opportunities afforded by the community for his talent in money making.

What would the talent of a Bell be worth and all the equipment of telephone companies in the wilds of Africa? Consequently, it may be said that a large part of the profits made by anyone is due to the environment in which he has been placed, that taken from this environment and put in another, no matter how great his talent he would never have the opportunity to make that much money. If this be the case, it is but natural to expect the successful to contribute to the upkeep of that government—which is the foundation of their environment—an earnest of what the government is worth to them.

We have realized all along that our taxation system is far from scientific. This system has grown loosely out of a number of experiences and emergencies and it certainly needs thorough overhauling. It is another example, antedating the New Deal, of generally poor planning. Tax measures are usually conceived in haste, under pressure of discovering new sources of revenue and by compromises with powerful interests or their lobbies.

Under the pressure of rising deficits and because of a government policy gradually to eliminate such deficits at a time when there is still a need for new expenditures, there has not been an opportunity to make the proper study. Furthermore, conditions are not propitious, in the early stages of recovery, for the introduction of a sounder system, because there are too many potential contributors to revenue who are still wobbling and more likely to require government support than to be able to support the government.

Among the accomplishments of the present administration which has brought forth much criticism, mention should be made of the Revenue Act of 1936. I believe that justifiable criticism can be urged, not only for the manner in which the original Tax Bill was presented, premising a new and unexpected theory of taxation; not only for the lack of supporting data for the provisions sought to be made into law; but also for some aspects of the statute as finally enacted by Congress. To be sure, tax legislation in an election year is not likely to be as objective as is legislative consideration of the same subject matter a year later. One must also keep in mind the fact that the legislative process inevitably reflects compromises of all sorts, some good and some bad. The scope of this volume will not permit me to deal in detail with the new Revenue Act.

However, I believe that the novelty of the approach in a matter of such a grave concern to American business requires that there be the most careful and expert study in order that so far as possible, the provisions of the law be rested upon a scientific basis. The time schedule of the present law, while in Congress, rendered such an inquiry impossible, and the evidence at the Congressional hearings revealed very clearly that there was lacking such necessary fundamental supporting data.

Finally, I believe the statute, even as presently enacted with a multitude of concessions to special circumstances deserving exemptive treatment, is premised upon a fallacious economic principle. As I view it, the underlying postulate of this statute is that net income is the equivalent of disbursable income, and that it is fair to tax disbursable income and to compel its disbursement by a heavy tax on the income not so disbursed. Space does not permit my detailing the numerous instances where prudent management would require that a sharp distinction be drawn between net income and that properly the subject of dividend declaration.

The adverse efforts of the new act are of course, a matter of prognosis. But it appears to me that the Revenue Act may result unfavorably to two types of corporations. First consider the company which has been hard hit by the depression and has been slow in recovery, and is now struggling to its feet. The compulsory change in the distribution policy of such a corporation which the introduction of the surtax on undivided profits is bound to bring about is likely to leave the company in an impaired condition from the view point of financial stability. Secondly, the company which is well off financially is now given a premium not to save. Its dividend policy will be of a hit or miss variety, depending on the fortunes of the year, and should another depression overtake us, it may find many such companies unprepared for a severe financial storm.

We must eventually achieve a fair, realistic and permanent tax program, non-punitive, politically or otherwise. It is to be hoped that the Administration will study scientifically the contributions of all sections of our economy to the upkeep of government—their invisible and indirect contributions as well as the actual taxes paid—to the end that a fair, equitable, and efficient distribution of the tax burden be established. Levies, above all, should be horizontal so that all who earn will, by a tax payment, however small, be made conscious of the fact that it costs money to be governed.

CHAPTER VIII

In Which a Planned Program is Defended and Planning is Defined

I

THE preceding discussion has analyzed the planning of the New Deal on only a few of the many fronts where goes the battle against this depression and its recurrence. As we try to appraise the future with these matters in mind, certain definite tendencies are certain, if the New Deal continues.

A constructively rehabilitated taxation system will make it possible for the government to take in progressively more income, while increased production will reduce the requirements for relief and PWA activities. The deficit will turn into a surplus and the government debt will again begin to contract and possibly, at the same time, shift to a greater proportion of the population. On the basis of a strong credit and banking structure, consciously controlled and coupled with many subsidiary measures like social security, a constructive agricultural policy, and a labor and industrial policy to cope with the problems of displacement and instability of tenure, we should be able to formulate and enact measures which will cushion us against depression, if and when it recurs. They will make us "depression-prepared."

If we continue in this direction we shall be ready, economically, financially and socially, to act rapidly with blue-prints drawn in advance. There is no other time to do this but now, when prosperity is returning. It is arrived prosperity that, in the past, has engendered crises.

If the New Deal goes along on these lines of planning for a generation or two, it may end depressions altogether. At least, it will eliminate some of the worst evils of depressions, provided, of course, that radical or conservative demagogues do not interfere with ordinary development. A sturdy adherence to the program of reform will ensure the America of tomorrow what it lacked so sadly yesterday—a reasonably adequate guarantee of security.

There is danger of recurrence of the depression. In the period from 1926 to 1929, with a much less difficult international trade situation, with a much smaller accumulation of unemployed, and with much smaller bank reserves, we were digging the worst economic pit the country ever troubled with. If we revert to Old Deal control of an administration, however benevolently headed, the depression will return; it is inherent in these philosophies and in its social techniques.

The New Deal had to design its own measures to bring about the present improvement. It has left important traces on our economic life and on the social consciousness of our people and a great part of it has become permanent in our economic structure. The New Deal program presupposes a continuity of protection on the part of the government, and hence there is a need of consolidating and finishing the job which is today only half done.

I have presented some of the factors which seem basic in any economic or social appraisal of the New Deal. But since political issues are becoming of greater importance to every one in our nation, it is necessary to weigh also the New Deal's political opposition and following.

The college or high school graduate cannot leave political issues to his elders, because today he is immediately faced with the problem of getting a job and sees the intimate relationship between his situation and the social order under which he lives. The men and women more than 50 years old, who often in this age of efficiency have no opportunity of continuing as wage earners, are vitally interested in our political structure. The farmer, the workingman, the white-collar clerk and small business men (for the larger and more powerful business interests have always been concerned with government) are all necessarily interested in our political affairs.

Opposing the New Deal is, first, that group which profited most under the Old Deal. Temporarily frightened in 1932, they have now recovered from this panic. They have forgotten how nearly they came to losing everything only a short time ago and do not admit that the New Deal has had any beneficial effects in stimulating recovery. They take recovery for granted and reason that, if they could in some manner get rid of the New Deal, they would have less taxes to pay, less regulation, and, in a word, could have their cake and eat it, too. Because of the power of their money, their influence is substantial, chiefly among white-collar workers and small business men who look up to them.[1] These latter groups, although they have only small incomes, are not direct beneficiaries of the New Deal. It made them share certain responsibilities for which their education and background had given them no preparation.

On an opposite front, the New Deal is assailed by melancholy radicals who want so many things, and want them all done overnight. Some of their aims are good, but any belief that they can be quickly accomplished has small place in the program of a realistic political party. But a part of this group merely wants to do away with the democratic order altogether. No debate with these is possible since their purpose is not to discuss but to destroy.

Two other groups whose hostility to Rooseveltian policies is very pronounced, ought perhaps, to be mentioned. They are termed the "Anti-Spenders" and the "Constitutionalists." These terms are not meant to represent groups sharply set off from the rest of the opposing citizenry, but rather as indicative of the

[1] The relation of this group to the press of the country should not be minimized. Sir Wilmott Lewis, Washington correspondent of the London Times, recently said at a luncheon of the Associated Press:

"Both in England and the United States the danger which confronts what we call the freedom of the press *is not chiefly from without,* for that we can meet, *but from within.* It is, as I see it, a danger which grows with the growth and with the increasing integration of the newspaper system—the danger that the freedom which makes us great and useful may make some among us too great; that individuals may acquire a power which (if the freedom we demand is to be ours) they cannot be prevented from harnessing *in the service of personal ambition* rather than *of the community* from which their strength flows." (Italics mine, J. P. K.)

type of argument advanced by each as the primary reason for their opposition to Mr. Roosevelt. A word about them.

The "Anti-Spenders" take the position that the program of Federal expenditures in whole or in large part represents a waste of public funds—that the economic maladjustment consequent upon the "Crash" were in the course of being cured when the President entered office—that his policy constituted interference not only increasing the public debt enormously, but also retarding a normal recovery.

Here, again, I wish to emphasize the importance of discriminating criticism. In many instances, the spending activities of the Administration are the subject of proper attack. Even when one takes into account the inevitable haste required by the emergency, the lack of a trained personnel, the tremendous though traditional political pressures, the lack of enlightening precedents, there is still a strong case to be made out for the opposition, in particular instances, on the score of wisdom, partisanship efficiency. But that the Federal Government should withdraw entirely from giving financial aid, or that the increase in Federal expenditures be but moderate, are theses no reputable economist could defend. The extraordinary expenditures began under Mr. Hoover, and, despite his sizable disbursements, the spiral of deflation continued unchecked. It requires no complex logical process to appreciate that an extraordinary depression required extraordinary remedies, including extraordinary expenditures.

One of the curious arguments is seen in the dogma of some of the "Anti-Spenders," who want the budget balanced and yet demand that government aid be extended to their particular group. It is too late to adopt a principle that the Federal Government is forbidden to help special groups as indirect aid to the general welfare. It is over 100 years too late. In fact, no one champions such an extreme view. That would indeed be a reversal of a traditional policy of the Federal Government almost since its inception. It is not the fact of spending per se, but the kind and method of spending which should concern us. Once again, I refer to the chaos the President found when he entered office. In the light of actualities and potentialities of danger to the very fabric of the social order, the "Anti-Spenders" have but a feeble argument.

Does anyone believe that the defeat of Mr. Roosevelt will end the problem of Federal expenditures and bring about a balanced budget? Should Mr. Roosevelt be defeated, disregarding the political differences which would inevitably result between the Senate and the Chief Executive, I would expect little change in the Federal fiscal problems, but great trouble if the policies of President Roosevelt were to be abandoned.

In no phase of the campaign against Mr. Roosevelt, is there more emotionalism, real and feigned, than in the appeal of the "Constitutionalists." I imagine that there are some people who honestly believe that the President seeks to overthrow Constitutional Government by covert means. For such as these no amount of argument would be availing. I know that many of these ardently professing their latter day faith in "States' Rights" and their zeal for the Constitution, know full well that the President has no designs on that eminent tribunal which "interprets" the supreme law of the land.

Certainly it cannot be argued that the court is above criticism. To advocate such a view would be to grant an immunity which would be the very negation of democracy. A lawyer, a politician, or a law teacher does not attain a state of infallibility by Presidential investiture. Is it not clear that a dissenting opinion is itself a criticism of the majority whose votes have decided the law at least for the time being? The history of this country records numerous controversies regarding the correctness, and, in numerous instances, the "fairness" of the Supreme Court's rulings. Lincoln in his first inaugural address, took sharp issue with the Highest Court, saying, "If the policy of the Government on vital questions affecting the whole people is to be irrevocably fixed by the decisions of the Supreme Court, the instant they are made in an ordinary litigation between parties in personal actions, the people will have ceased to be their own rulers, having to that extent practically resigned their government into the hands of that eminent tribunal."

The differences about the Constitution and its interpretation should not give us great concern. It is the natural result of the newness of the New Deal. If the American people want the policies advocated by the President to prevail, they shall prevail, and in an orderly, peaceful, and constitutional manner. And this despite the reign of horror conjured up by the "Constitutionalists," whose opposition, if the truth were known, is more mundane and selfish than the ideals of patriotism and human welfare in the name of which they protest.

These are the elements arrayed against the New Deal. To offset them it has the support of those who believe that solutions in modern civilization require conscious control and who want such control to take place under a democratic mechanism. They contend that, in a civilization where much of our daily lives is based on contractual relationships—what may be called a paper civilization—there is need for control. They hold further that, while formerly our economy may have been able to adjust itself to any stresses because of the underlying trend of rapid growth, now, with a slower rate of growth, such self-adjustment is too painful. There is no longer any acceleration in the rate of growth; and the slower pace means adjustments in our debt and credit structure; in our Federal and state taxation. Briefly, it means planning. The New Deal is more than a crystallization of the economic needs of the country; it is also the spirit of modern America. Its supporters appreciate that President Roosevelt, in his search for social justice, is comparable to an unselfish scientist who sacrifices time and energy to seek health for the masses.

CHAPTER IX

In Which the Origin and Effect of the Federal Securities Legislation are Discussed

I

AMONG the many matters discussed by the President during the course of his pre-election campaign were the problems of the investor in securities, with particular relation to the powers of the Federal Government to furnish protection. On August 20, 1932, at Columbus, Ohio, the President indicated his general point of view as to the situation of the defrauded investor. While the stock market boiled and prosperity appeared to be a permanent part of the American national life, there was little thought given to the national nature of the problems of the security business. True, great losses had been suffered by investors throughout the country because of deceit in the sale of securities. Many states were extremely active in their attempts to prevent the manifold practices of defrauding investors. However, it was not until the collapse of 1929, when the stock market tickers revealed how ephemeral were the values upon which we had based our standard of living, that the American people began to envisage the magnitude of the problems of investors, the helplessness of the individual shareholders, the inadequacy of the existing modes of control and the vital necessity for Federal action.

The demand for congressional action arose partly because of the large interstate fraudulent sales of securities, which state action but feebly checked; partly from continually increasing pressure for some device to compel disclosure, sponsored by a respectable and important group in the financial community. These people had made it their profession to furnish financial information about corporations and to advise on the merits of the security. Such organizations as Moody's and Standard Statistics, which had developed large, efficient and expensive organizations for assembling corporate data, very frequently had to resort to surmise in arriving at their views on many important companies. It was impossible in many cases to ascertain fundamental facts about companies whose securities were held by the public. The management refused to make available necessary information. So, also, with investment counsellors, the lack of candid disclosure was a serious factor, minimizing the effectiveness of their judgment.

It is generally agreed that America became a nation of investors as a direct result of the Liberty Loan drives during the World War. Prior to that time there was a slow but orderly growth in the number of American investors, but the number of American rails and industrials still listed on the London Stock Exchange proves that the early financing of American business originally was effected to a great extent in foreign markets. The widespread public participation in the distribution of Liberty Bonds, necessary in order to finance the War, first taught the American people generally to think of ownership of property in terms of ownership of securities, so that non-governmental financing after the War was marked by a tremendous increase in the number of public offerings.

As might have been expected, this increase in investment interest proved to be a fertile source of profit for knaves. Swindling apace, and the frauds practised on investors attained gigantic proportions. The Committee on Banking and Currency of the Senate, in reporting the Securities Act of 1933, estimated that the losses to the public from investments in practically worthless securities had aggregated $1,700,000,000 annually. While data of this kind are not very reliable, everyone who has studied the problem agrees that investors' losses through fraudulent sales of securities had reached staggering proportions and were, to a large extent, avoidable through proper supervision.

Since 1911, the states have been aware of the growing evil of security frauds. In that year was passed the first Blue Sky Act. Within the next two decades similar legislation was enacted in nearly all the states of the Union. The method adopted by the states varied somewhat. Some states provided for the registration of brokers and dealers; others required registration of the securities; and still others made precedent to sale that a state commission grant said approval of the investment merits of a security. While much good resulted from this type of control, and, doubtless, thousands of investors were enabled to avoid imposition, the fact remains that the security frauds continued to be a serious national problem. One reason for the ineffectiveness of state action can be appreciated when one considers the technique of a large scale fraudulent operation. The sales originate in State A, but the victims solicited reside in other States. Thus, by mail and more frequently by telephone, security sales are negotiated to the detriment of innocent purchasers who must go to another jurisdiction to make effective complaint. Frequently the act complained of was not a crime in the state of origin. Even if the action were criminal, the pressure upon prosecuting officials was not as great as if the sale had been made to a local resident.

A conclusive demonstration that state blue-sky legislation, however efficiently and honestly enforced, was not adequate to meet the problem of securities frauds was made by the National Association of Securities Commissioners at their annual meeting in 1924. These were the men charged with the duty of enforcing the laws of the several states; yet, after considering the case of protecting the investor, they passed a resolution acknowledging the inability of the states to control the evils and advocating Federal blue sky legislation to supplement the laws of the states. Thus, even prior to President Roosevelt's election we had a history of securities frauds in this country and a slowly-developing demand for governmental action. The stock-market crash finally crystallized sentiment in favor of a Federal securities act.

2

Congress had many alternatives before it in 1933 when considering securities legislation. It could have required approval by a bureau as a condition to the use of the mails. It could have imposed a license system. It could have adopted other alternatives.

Congress, however, refrained from extreme legislation. It passed an act which is very simple in scope and which cuts to a minimum the risk of bureaucratic control. Although the statute itself makes it a crime to declare that registration of a security means the Commission has approved it, and although the text clearly demonstrates that Congress intended only to require truthful disclosure, it is surprising how many intelligent people still believe that the Securities and Exchange Commission must approve the investment merits of a security prior to its valid sale. The President himself in the message transmitting the bill to the Congress indicated the nature of the legislation, the problems sought to be solved, and also a path of comprehensive reform in this field:

"I recommend to the Congress legislation for Federal supervision of traffic in investment securities in interstate commerce.

"In spite of many State statutes the public in the past has sustained severe losses through practices neither ethical nor honest on the part of many persons and corporations selling securities.

"Of course, the Federal Government cannot and should not take any action which might be construed as approving or guaranteeing that newly issued securities are sound in the sense that their value will be maintained or that the properties which they represent will earn profit.

"There is, however, an obligation upon us to insist

that every issue of new securities to be sold in interstate commerce shall be accompanied by full publicity and information, and that no essentially important element attending the issue shall be concealed from the buying public.

"This proposal adds to the ancient rule of caveat emptor, the further doctrine 'let the seller also beware.' It puts the burden of telling the whole truth on the seller. It should give impetus to honest dealing in securities and thereby bring back public confidence.

"The purpose of the legislation I suggest is to protect the public with the least possible interference to honest business."

This Act, which is far less burdensome in many particulars than the statute providing for postal fraud orders, was passed without a dissenting vote by Congress. Immediately, there began an organized campaign which is significantly similar to the campaign against the President. No statement was too extreme in condemning this legislation. Lawyers who should have known better made it appear that the theory of liability adopted was unknown to the Anglo-American code of law. Directors were induced to believe that filing a registration statement was like signing as the maker of a promissory note, payable to any member of the public. The collapse of the capital security market, always regarded as an inevitable incident of a depression, was attributed exclusively to the liability sections of the securities legislation. The folly of this contention was exposed in the "Midland Bank Monthly Review" (July-August, 1934) where it was pointed out that new issues are always scarce in times of depression because neither issuers nor investors care to take on new risks in a period of great unsettlement.

Much of the hostile talk about the Securities Act has by this time disappeared. The record of registrations makes such condemnation appear foolish on its face. Yet only the other day at a Senate hearing, a prominent economist repeated the old bromide that we would now have recovery but for the Securities Act.

Purposely, I do not enter into extended discussion regarding the manifest error of the charges against the President because of this legislation. My main point is to show that the Act represents a minimum protection for the public whose money is sought for private enterprise. The least the public is entitled to know is the truth about the enterprise, its financial condition, the purposes for which the proceeds are to be used, the amount of promoters' profits, the underwriting commissions, etc. The fact is that the investment fraternity have come to regard the Securities Act as a sound piece of legislation representing a proper balance between protection to be accorded to the helpless and freedom for individual enterprise. A very short time ago one of the most prominent figures in the investment banking fraternity informed me that the repeal or judicial invalidation of the Federal securities legislation would be a definite defeat of the decent elements in American business life.

It is interesting to note that a Royal Commission in Canada whose corporate problems are, if anything, less serious than ours, has considered carefully the problems of the investor and corporate control and has recommended legislation which is substantially equivalent to the Securities Act of 1933. I believe it is safe to say that Federal legislation which requires the disclosure of essential facts, as does this Act, and which imposes appropriate civil and criminal sanctions can meet any fair-minded test for sound government. The problem is national; the approach is prudent; and the method adopted is reasonably calculated to bring about the desired objectives.

3

When the Senate Committee on Banking and Currency began its investigation into stock exchange practices in 1932 none could have forseen that its revelations would be so startling. It was impossible to have previsioned the extent to which the American public had been imposed upon by unfair practices and fradulent schemes of all sorts. For month after month the country was treated to a series of amazing revelations which involved practically all the important names in the financial community in practices which, to say the least, were highly unethical. The belief that those in control of the corporate life of America were motivated by honesty and ideals of honorable conduct was completely shattered. The rising wrath of the American people made inevitable the further

extension of Federal control in order to prevent the
abuses on the organized exchanges and in the over-the-
counter markets of the country.

Here again, there had been a history of a constantly
growing demand for Federal supervision. As far back
as 1910 there had been an attempt to bring the securities markets within the jurisdiction of the Federal
government. The famous Pujo inquiry, which preceded the establishment of the Federal Reserve System, also produced a demand for Federal regulation of
stock exchanges. The Securities Exchange Act of 1934,
which created the Commission on which I served, was
the logical successor of these early attempts at Federal
regulation and was dictated, section by section, by
the testimony of the witnesses who appeared before
the Senate Committee. Washed sales, matched orders,
market rigging and other forms of manipulation, trading by insiders, inadequate margins, withholding material information in reports and proxies, abuses in
short selling, and a host of other abuses, were recognized and provided for in the statute. Running to
form, unthinking reactionaries forced the Act to run a
gauntlet of organized propaganda. It was assailed as
state socialism and regimentation; and, in accordance
with the custom of parading imaginary horribles, it
was prophesied that the securities markets of the
country would dry up within a few months. These
critics forgot that a substantially similar scheme of
preventing manipulation on grain markets of the
country was enacted in 1922 as the Grain Futures Act,
and that the grain markets have continued to function

effectively since that time. Similarly here, despite all the dismal forebodings, the Securities Exchange Act was put into operation and has been received with acclaim by the majority of persons concerned.

It is not my purpose here to enter into a detailed discussion of the provisions of the Securities Act of 1933 or the Securities Exchange Act of 1934, or of the administration which these statutes have received from the Securities and Exchange Commission. But it so happens that this Commission is the only agency of the government with which I have been connected under President Roosevelt, and I feel that some explanation of the operations of this Commission may be helpful in meeting certain accusations against the President.

The charge is made frequently that the President has built up a vast machinery for patronage, and that the Civil Service reforms, hardly won after many years of struggle, have been betrayed. This is certainly not true of the Securities and Exchange Commission, of the Federal Communications Commission, of the enlarged Federal Power Commission, Agricultural Adjustment Administration, Farm Credit Administration, National Labor Relations Board, Railroad Retirement Board, Social Security Board, and others. Only those agencies which were created for the immediate purpose of promoting recovery were exempted from the Civil Service laws.

Of course, in the case of the Securities and Exchange Commission, certain expert personnel were exempted from Civil Service examination, although in all other respects they were classified Civil Service employees. This was a Congressional recognition of the difficulty of securing expert personnel in a highly technical field.

4

Another charge often made against the administration of President Roosevelt is that he has entrusted the administration of his reform legislation to hopeless visionaries—men without practical experience in the field where they are administering, and unwilling to accept any suggestions from people with experience. How is this charge borne out at the offices of the Securities and Exchange Commission? While I can never hope to lay claim to being a definitive authority on the securities business, I do not recall that I was ever accused of lacking practical experience in that trade. Criticism of me at the time of my appointment more frequently charged that I had too much practical experience and that I was unsympathetic with the reforms sought to be achieved by the new laws. I prefer to let the record of the Commission testify to my sympathy with this legislation and to say a word about the other Commissioners who served with me, each of whom contributed so much to the administration of the Commission.

It must be remembered that the Commission was charged with administering and enforcing two laws, and that these laws, while simple enough in their purposes, as I have already indicated, were complex in their administration and enforcement because of the very complexity of the business affected by them. Consequently, it was necessary that lawyers should predominate in the Commission in order that the fundamental nature of the regulations should be exactly interpreted. The significance of President Roosevelt's appointments to the Commission lies not so much in the fact that he appointed lawyers, as in the type of lawyers whom he appointed.

James M. Landis had been Professor of Legislation in the Harvard Law School and one of the outstanding authorities in the country on the interpretation and application of statutes. He had been closely connected with the preparation of both the statutes under which we are working and intimately familiar with the history of these statutes in Congress and the interpretation given them by Congress. He had been a Commissioner of the Federal Trade Commission and in that capacity his was the difficult task of supervising the administration of the Securities Act during the first year of its operation. His specialized skill in the preparation of regulations having the force of statutes were indispensable for a Commission which necessarily operated through such rules and regulations.

Another Commissioner was Robert E. Healy who for many years prior to his appointment had been Chief Counsel to the Federal Trade Commission. Thus he brought to the new Securities and Exchange Commission an intimate knowledge of the problems connected with the administration and enforcement of the Securities Act of 1933, together with a practical

working knowledge of the whole controversial field
of administrative law. His handling of the Federal
Trade Commission's investigation into the operations
of public utility holding companies was a masterpiece
of careful and painstaking work in an involved subject extending over many years. His findings in this
investigation, more than any other single factor, contributed to the enactment of the Public Utility Holding Company Act of 1935; and his experience gained
from this investigation was of inestimable value to
the new Commission which had for one of its principal
functions complex investigations in the securities
field. Ferdinand Pecora came directly to the Commission from the investigation of stock exchange practices which resulted in the Securities Exchange Act.
He had been counsel to the Senate Committee on
Banking and Currency, and more than any other man
in the country he had at his fingertips a knowledge of
the abuses which the Securities Exchange Act had
been enacted to prevent. George C. Mathews, another
of the original Commissioners was not a lawyer. He
had behind him many years of experience in business,
and, what was even of greater importance, many years
of experience in the administration of the Wisconsin
securities laws, which are generally regarded as the
most forward-looking of all state blue sky legislation.

I have worked with these men intimately many
hours a day for six days a week and it is my considered opinion that a more balanced group for the
new Commission could not have been found.

The Commission necessarily recognized that the reforms had to be effected without dislocating the existing financial machinery of the country. In a sense they were watchmakers told to repair and correct a clock while that clock continued to run, and one need not be a watchmaker to conceive the difficulty of this task.

The Commission first surrounded itself with a staff whose competence has never been challenged. Lawyers, accountants, technical trading experts, research men, all were drawn to Washington, not so much on their own applications as the result of search for the best available personnel. It is a tribute to these men and the Commission which selected them that they came willingly and even eagerly, particularly the younger men, who were anxious to participate in the creation of this New Deal for the investing public at a time when their elders were content to sit back and criticize.

With its staff organized, the Commission did not embark on any campaign to instill fear into the securities business. It realized that the most effective enforcement of the Acts would follow from the coöperation of people in the business. In the preparation of its forms and regulations, in drafting rules governing trading on exchanges, in considering the problems of the industry generally, no important step was taken without fully discussing it with those persons who would be affected. The interplay of ideas brought out in such conferences ironed out all essential differences between the industry and the Commission, so that I can honestly say that every constructive step which the Commission has taken accords with the

letter and spirit of the legislation and is supported
by a respectable majority of the industry as a whole.

When the Commissioners entered upon their task
Federal securities legislation, however, badly needed,
was an untried experiment; yet in two short years it
has become an accepted commonplace in the financial
business of the country, appreciatively hailed by business and the public alike.

It is my considered judgment that when the economic crisis which began in 1929 is dim in history, the
Acts providing for the regulation of public offerings of
securities and for the control of trading on the stock
exchanges and in the over-the-counter markets will
still be regarded as two of the most beneficial statutes
enacted in years. Who can doubt that, if similar
statutes had been in effect in 1920, billions of dollars
would have been saved to innocent investors, the excessive speculation of the Twenties would have been
impossible, the credit inflation lessened and the staggering burden of debt in large part avoided?

CHAPTER X

In Which the President is Shown as the Real Defender of American Freedom

I

ONE critic, attacking the administration of President Roosevelt, dramatically proclaims:

"Our country is faced with a crisis more serious than any mere 'depression.'

"It is faced by a question more basic than unemployment or low prices or heavy debts.

"When you and I go to the polls in November 1936 we shall be voting, not for any one man, not for any one party, not for any one remedy or group of remedies, but for the continuance or discontinuance of the freedom we have enjoyed under what for want of a better name we call the American scheme of life."

One would assume that this over-stimulated critic would have compared the experiences in this country with those of the world at large. Had he done so, he would have been compelled to note the usurpation by dictators of power over life and liberty in one foreign nation after another and the gradual imposition of serfdom upon distant people. If, instead of indulging in hysterics, he had analyzed the underlying causes of this tendency toward tyranny abroad, he would have ascertained that unemployment of the masses of people was disintegrating the cornerstones of democracy, that, because of unemployment, dictators were able to

cause the complete collapse of the structure of
freedom.

Unemployment, increased and accentuated by the
trend of world politics and industrial evolution—unemployment which destroyed the morale of nations
and beclouded the reasoning of people—this was the
Achilles heel of freedom and liberty.

Straight-thinking people know that unemployment
is the root of all the ills and ailments of subjugated
people of Europe. The critics of the Roosevelt administration, who so loudly and devoutly profess
their unswerving belief in democracy, refuse, for reasons best known to themselves, to support the administration's attempt to obliterate unemployment, the
greatest threat and menace to our institutions of
freedom.

Are they to be the modern Bourbons who never
learn? They have already forgotten the lesson of the
past five years. With the release, through the unre-
mitting efforts of the Roosevelt administration, of the
tension of unemployment and distress, came relief of
mind, but also the resumption of unthinking aggres-
siveness among those who catapulted our nation into
an economic morass.

Democracy will not be safe for this country unless
we constructively deal with causes of dictatorships.
Planned action is imperative, or else capitalism and
the American scheme of life will be in serious jeop-
ardy. The necessity for a comprehensive program to
solve the problem of unemployment of the aged and
young, to restore the farmer to economic security, to

strengthen the financial and industrial fiber of our country, has been indelibly imprinted on the mind and memory of our people. The Republican platform of 1936 is a marked, grudging admission of this.

The cure for democracy is faith in democracy, a faith founded on economic and social security, a faith unshaken by the stress and turmoil of hunger and unemployment.

The fundamental importance of the depression and unemployment cannot be lightly dismissed. The continuance or discontinuance of freedom is the vital issue of the presidential election of 1936. Freedom not only embraces political, civil and religious liberty but also the economic security which is an integral and basic component of real and lasting freedom. What matters a vote to a hungry man? If our democracy is to survive the attacks of dictatorship, whether open or veiled, we must solve the problem of security.

The miseries of depression and unemployment overshadowed the thoughts of the working man plodding the streets; the young man and woman despairing of employment; the farmer laboring to produce grain and losing a quarter of a dollar on every bushel; the home-owner whose home was threatened with foreclosure; and every other citizen to whom depression meant strangulation. These were the pathological spots in the American scheme of life which had to be removed if democracy was to survive. Refusing to recognize the diagnosis was no cure.

The development of modern democracies has been the result of deprivation of license and privilege of

the few, with a resultant increase of freedom for the
many. From the olden days of the Industrial Revolution, when feudal lords were deprived of their right
to exploit their serfs, to the time when income taxes
were first introduced, alarmists proclaimed their loss
of freedom. Progress and reformation, in every land,
has been regarded by those who were favored by the
ancient régime as an infringement on freedom. The
emancipation of the people politically, as well as economically, was always resisted by the "warders of
freedom."[1]

The lesson of the last few years is clear—every dictatorship in a foreign country walked into power over
a bridge built by false liberals, who bemoaned their
lost liberties and united against the "oppression and
tyranny" of their then existing governments.

The farmer, the working man, and the large middle
classes of the United States will know that their freedom has not been impaired under Mr. Roosevelt. The
farmer knows that the one "freedom" he did lose was
the freedom of being a victim of agricultural chaos—
chaos which rendered his labor, his crops and his
property worthless. The working man knows that
the one "freedom" he did lose was the "freedom" of
being a commodity in a tremendously over-supplied
labor market—a labor market which at times compelled him to work at a wage of a few cents an hour.
The one "freedom" the worker will not regret losing

[1] As Governor Alf M. Landon conceded in his address to the Methodist
District Conference at Greeley, Colo., March 29, 1935.

is the freedom of a declining standard of living and of a steadily declining bargaining power.

The Roosevelt administration has restored the confidence of our people in democracy by a conscious intervention into the economic forces of our national life. As a consequence, the laborer, the working man, the farmer, the home-owner and no less the banker, the financier and the industrialist were lifted from political and economic darkness into the light of political and economic freedom. The task of the administration has not been completed. What has already been done to make the democratic order more stable, secure and efficient offers to the average man the hope that the up-trend of today may have greater permanence than when it was a mere cyclical rebound.

2

But the critics go a step further and intimate that the President, whatever the effects of his program on the economic mechanism, has set up or is tending to set up a dictatorial order, more or less along the lines of the dictatorships in Europe. This general contention has been discussed above. There is no doubt that as we approach economic security, then only do we approach real freedom. Nevertheless, this argument may be further analyzed.

Of course, in the first place, this argument is a method by which to avoid an earnest discussion of the fundamental aspects of the present economic and social life and to resort, instead, to appeals to the superstitions and prejudices of the uninformed. The dishonesty of the attack is apparent. How potently insincere it is to compare the efforts of Mr. Roosevelt to bring order out of chaos within the framework of a democracy, to the activities of a Stalin, a Hitler, or a Mussolini, whose first steps were to do away with democratic machinery. To characterize an administration under which government ownership of industry is practically non-existent, an administration which has avoided and resisted government ownership, as of socialistic or dictatorial nature, is a flagrant distortion of the truth. Small wonder that the great majority of the nation lost confidence in a financial system dominated by such "leaders."

The New Deal is founded upon a basic belief in the efficacy of the capitalistic system. Every effort has been strained to preserve the system. It believes neither in state nor private socialism. It does believe, however, that the beneficiaries of a prosperous democracy should, in fairness to everybody and in their own interest, contribute in the form of taxes and social responsibility the equivalent of what an organized, prosperous and stable democratic community is worth to them. Certain of the President's critics have no sincere interest in a better "state," no honest desire to clean up the "unholy mess," beyond salvaging the interests which they control. The "state" which they apparently wanted to strengthen was the "state" of a comparative handful of privileged aristocrats. In their blind adherence to outmoded principles, they lose sight of their own longer-term interests. For it is fundamental that in the prosperity of all classes lies the security of their possessions.

Clearly this administration is for a certain degree of regulation, and it is regulated individualism. But this is a necessary step, if we are to avoid real dictatorship and real loss of freedom. The question today is whether we should intelligently regulate our social life so as to assure the maintenance of a democracy, or should smash our regulatory machine and thus pave the way for dictatorship. Should we try to have a balance between regulation and individualism, or should we revert to an uncontrolled individualistic scheme?

No civilized community ever existed without restraints. There is nothing revolutionary about President Roosevelt's philosophy. He is merely continuing a long established evolutionary trend of balance between individualism and social control. He is trying to retain the good things inherent in our individualistic system and, by regulation, rid the system of those aspects which spell self-destruction. Control and discipline are indispensable to any orderly society, just as they are part of the character of any well-bred individual. The acid test is to compare the net results and benefits to the average man under the "Old Deal" and under the "New Deal."

Under which régime will the masses fare better? Must they live under a system where adversity leaves them helpless and desolate without the comforting thought that the government will take some little care of them? Must they live under a system where adversity grants the freedom of committing suicide, or shall they seek lasting security? Because the critics may not believe with the President that much can be done to improve the lot of the people, does that cast a reflection on the President?

The bitter irony of this phase of the attack against the President is that, if the people are deluded by the outpourings of those who shout for "an end of the Roosevelt dictatorship," their victory will be Pyrrhic and they will have opened the gate for a real dictator, unless the general objectives of the President are pursued. The nation cannot undergo another attack of depression even approximating the one from which we are just emerging. Eternal vigilance is the price of liberty. What preparations do these critics advocate to forestall another catastrophe?

Should such a depression come under a government, unprepared for such an emergency, will the masses believe as readily as they did in the past that their chosen President and members of Congress will further their interests and incorporate their ideas and philosophies into our social life through appropriate legislation?

Will the masses still have faith in the peaceful democratic process, or will they have learned that their representatives may be helpless against the power of money which can produce insincere but politically effective propaganda?

May not the farmer then meditate that ours is a strange society in which the industrial corporation may attempt to keep production within the absorptive capacity of its market, but it is a sin for the farmer to do likewise? A farmer convinced that limitation of production is fundamentally the only method of solving his problem of over-production, in the absence of any other offered plan, may well think of means other than peaceful legislation for a solution of his ills. Shall we forget the Farm Holiday movement in 1933? The judge flung from his bench and roped around the neck in orderly Iowa?

May not the wage-earner, with the consciousness that the efforts to formulate a constructive labor and industrial policy have been thwarted by the organized efforts of industrialists, Chambers of Commerce and other similar agencies, rebel against a system which permits the few to destroy the safeguards against maximum hours of work and wages, child labor, stabilization of annual income, etc.?

If the white-collar workers, professionals and middle classes, as a result of conditions over which they have no control, cannot expect the government, duly elected by them, to help them in their hour of distress, then may they not lose interest in such a government and in the freedom which they only academically possess?

If the people of the country as consumers, producers and investors cannot find a way to protect their interests through the instrumentality of the ballot, may they not devise other means to obtain their objective?

The problems of today are beyond the stage of solution by any form of individualism. It is social democracy or what?

Certain it is that should reactionaries step in and, under whatever cover of "doing the same thing better," begin undoing the accomplishments of the New

Deal, they will destroy the present harmony existing between various classes. President Roosevelt has succeeded in uniting the interests of farmers, laborers and the mass of business men by *demonstrating the interdependence of their interests*. An awakened people can no longer be deluded with talk of rugged individualism as conducive to the social welfare.

The answer is that in Roosevelt lies the hope of real freedom for the mass of the people of the United States. The course which the President has pursued indicates this. It has not been a policy of concentrating on re-election by inaction and a laissez-faire attitude. Instead, the President, animated by a desire to bring to a successful culmination the task of rebuilding the collapsed structure of our nation, has pushed forward. Without indulging in vain promises, he continues regardless of the feeble outbursts of the willful obstructionists. The task has been begun and progress has been made. These actions are the complete refutation of the reckless charge that he is "Hell-Bent for Election." His aims are far more lasting. He would like to build a foundation for real and permanent freedom. Are we then to turn back at the crucial moment? Are we to abandon the sacred undertaking to bring to our people peace and security? Are we to return to the days of despair, uncertainty and confusion?

CHAPTER XI

In Which Ante-Election Pledges are Examined in the Light of Unforeseeable Events

I

THE President and his administration have been attacked because they have broken promises—because they have not followed the Democratic platform of 1932. It is charged they have not conformed to the Constitution.

Such criticism discloses, first, an unwillingness to judge the present administration plainly on its accomplishments and their effects on our social and economic structures; and, second, a vacuum of constructive suggestions which it requires a smoke screen to hide.

It is unintelligent to compare an administration's performance merely with a party platform on the theory that the platform represents a covenant between the candidate and those who voted for him. If a party program were all that counted in an election, then people would vote solely on the program and let each party committee select the Presidential candidates. But a party platform is only one of several factors which foreshadow the probable future action of the elected man.

It may truthfully be said that the candidate's speeches during the campaign have a much larger circulation than the party program and are more relied upon by the electorate. The speeches represent the candidate's personal views and are intended to be an account of the details in working out a formula.

As an indication of the vagueness of the planks in an election platform, we quote from the 1932 Democratic platform: "Effective control of crop surpluses so that all farmers may have the full benefit of the domestic market. Enactment of every constitutional measure that will aid the farmer to receive for basic farm commodities, prices in excess of cost of production." This is a formula, and eight months or a year later it was necessary for someone to interpret it in the light of the emergency of the day and the outlook at that time if it was to become alive and effective. This is precisely what the AAA, in spite of certain possible mistakes, attempted to do. To say now that a plan evolved under this program is a breach of the platform, merely because, in its detailed outline, it was not described in one of the planks, is to doom every election program to remain a dead letter, a meaningless document.

Among other important bases of electoral choice are the personalities and backgrounds of the candidates. Background is not largely indicated by what the candidate thought, or felt, or said when he was at high school, at college, but by what he said when he offered himself before the people, what he said about the issues at the time of his election. Hence his speeches become more important and more vital as the event of election nears, because there he has a chance to react to the latest social, political and economic developments, as well as to the cross-current

of political thoughts and criticisms, and to tell the
people how he would act were he in the White House.

The really important period is that between nomi-
nation and election. Then the candidate has an opportunity to measure the situation and the various problems, not merely as an outsider, but as one who within
a short period may be called to be chief executive of
his country. His executive philosophy is being forged
under the fire of campaign battles, although if he re-
cants on principle he violates the privilege which
allows any honest man to change mere views, based
on a different set of facts.

President Roosevelt in 1932 did more than intimate.
He gave, not inklings, but a program, as the following
excerpts from his campaign speeches indicate. On September 14, 1932, at Topeka, Kansas, in discussing the
farm problem, he spoke of the "seamless web" of
economic life, the inter-dependence of industry and
agriculture, asserting that "industrial prosperity can
reach only artificial and temporary heights as it did
in 1929, if at the same time there is no agricultural
prosperity," and suggesting "first, I would reorganize
the Department of Agriculture and I would do it with
the purpose of building up a *program of national planning.* Second, I favor a definite policy of looking *toward the planned use of land.*" The candidate also spoke
about the immediate necessity "to provide a means
for bringing about through government effort, a substantial reduction in the difference between the prices
of things the farmer sells and the things the farmer
buys." In that speech he gave, in a general way, a

sketch of what later came to be known as the AAA policy.

Did those who cry "broken promises" fail to read the speech made by Mr. Roosevelt in San Francisco, September 23, 1932, in which the social philosophy of the New Deal was rather clearly outlined?

"Our Government formal and informal, political and economic, owes to everyone an avenue to possess himself of a portion of that plenty sufficient for his needs through his own work. . . . If in accord with this principle we must restrict the operations of the speculator, the manipulator, even the financier, I believe we must accept the restriction as needful *not to hamper individualism, but to protect it.* . . . They (the responsible heads of finance and industry) must, where necessary, sacrifice this or that private advantage and in reciprocal self-denial must seek a general advantage; it is here that formal government—political government if you choose—comes in."

Let me also recall the speech of September 21, 1932, at Portland, Oregon, where the power program was outlined and summarized:

"I have spoken of a 'new deal' for the American people. I believe that the 'new deal' can be applied very definitely to the relationship between the electric utilities on the one side and the consumer and the investor on the other. . . ."

And the general statement of Mr. Roosevelt's concept of the duty of the President, as stated in Sioux City on September 29, 1932:

"I conceive the Presidency not merely as an agency in which routine executive powers are exercised, but as a position of leadership in which may be wielded an influence for the general good of our American system of government. No other official except the Vice-President is elected by all the people of the country. No other official owes such a direct responsibility to all the people of the country. He is the responsible spokesman of the nation's policies and the nation's ideals. . . ."

and again, his statements as to the functions of government in Chicago, October 2, 1932,

"Government of all kinds must systematically eliminate special advantages, eliminate special favors, eliminate special privileges wherever possible—whether they come, my friends, from tariff subsidies, or credit-favoritism, or taxation or anywhere else. . . ."

In Milwaukee, a day earlier, he had disclosed the philosophy he subsequently practiced.

". . . government not only must protect the rights of the individual by maintaining an interest in economic life, but it must extend the hand of aid and comfort whenever human values are at stake. . . ."

However, even the speeches made during the campaign do not represent a program which is to be adhered to literally six months later, when conditions may have changed fundamentally. Everyone changes his views (though not on the same set of facts, if he is worthy) as conditions change. The very process of learning consists merely of changing one's mind as one absorbs more facts and knows more about the subjects he is studying. It is not the act of changing one's views that counts. The validity of any change must be judged rather by the reasons for it and by the inherent merits of the new course of action as against the old. Of all the people in the nation, the President should least be expected to have a closed mind.

Now at the very eve of the Presidential election there is much ado about the 1932 platform of the Democratic party and an alleged betrayal of trust somewhat as though the platform was a legal document binding the candidate inflexibly for the term of his office. Yet nothing is said about the Congressional elections of 1934.

When the people of this country went to the polls in November of that year they could look back on an experience of over a year and a half of the New Deal and the leadership of President Roosevelt. In 1934 America had an opportunity to express a judgment in favor or against the program of the President. Then if ever was the time to cry pre-election "broken pledges." The country had if anything a sharper memory of presidential commitments. What happened is history.

The country gave the President and his policies thundering approval and elected a Congress overwhelmingly committed to the social objectives which the President has consistently and courageously sought to attain. It is very difficult in view of this undeniable verdict for me to see upon what basis the President can be charged with inconsistency. I think an impregnable case could be made out against the President at the source of broken promises, pledges, etc., if in the face of the electorate mandate of 1934, he had espoused different causes or had embraced the discredited theories of his critics.

An intelligent person knows that nobody can foresee everything the future may hold in store. When in March, 1933, the banks clamored for a holiday, and when at their insistence the President closed all the banks, which would have been closed anyway by the growing runs of depositors, he did the right thing. Similarly, in the droughts of 1934 and 1936, the movement of people and cattle from places where they would have perished, to places that were unaffected by the drought was necessary. It would have been a betrayal of the President's function not to have done the plain thing dictated by the circumstances and it would have been sheer pretense to hesitate on the ground that these things were not included in the party program or in the President's speeches. The same is true of the emergency aid to farm owners, through the mortgage moratorium.

The President, it may be repeated, is elected largely with the understanding that he is to have latitude of action. This is absolutely essential to efficient performance of his duty. We elect primarily the *man* who is not only free to make changes but also bound to make them as they are dictated by circumstances and emergencies. A President cannot refer to his campaign program as a series of statutes inescapably to be applied, because situations will arise neither foreseen nor forseeable at the time the program was drawn up. It is simply a guiding chart.

A worthy President cannot say, for example, if all the banks are closing, or if foreclosures of homes and farm property are making the nation homeless, or if the flood of unemployment is threatening to inundate our whole social structure, that he cannot do anything about these things because no provisions were made in the platform for financing such acts. He cannot excuse his failure to suggest a temporary halt in such foreclosures, a moratorium, because the party program has not provided for it. It will be remembered, in this connection, that in 1931 President Hoover, under the pressure of a very difficult international financial situation, suggested a moratorium on international debts, although such action was never conceived in party platform or presidential program or caucus. It is the specific duty of the President as an executive to supply leadership within constitutional limitations, and it is his duty to ask Congress to do the thing which, under the circumstances, seems to be the most appropriate thing to do.

One may go even further and say that unless the executive branch of the government is given, in the future, a greater latitude of action, and develops a technique of greater cooperation with the legislative branch, democracy will remain at a disadvantage in point of resiliency, flexibility and general efficiency, as compared with dictatorial forms of government.

Possibly one of the greatest political contributions of President Roosevelt has been the vindication of democracy as an efficient political instrument that can act swiftly and decisively, and powerfully and constructively, without sacrificing any of the substance of democracy.

2

Consider the promises of the President and the manner in which the accomplishments of the administration should be compared with these promises. The President pledged economy, and did in fact immediately take steps toward achieving such economy upon taking office. He reduced government salaries, because this was a logical step to bring compensation to this group of employees into line with cost of living. However, he increased government expenditures when he began from a necessitous new position his attack against depression, and, as we have indicated, these expenditures have been more than justified by the results.

Can we cry "broken promises" because of the mortgage moratorium, promulgated at a time when the situation had reached such intensity that lives of officers of the law were in danger, and at a time when the sheer folly of attempting to arrest deflation by permitting the worst form of deflation was evident? There is no theory of American political life that adherence to a program which had been announced during a campaign is required in the face of circumstances of peril not present at the time of the promise. These instances indicate that there are circumstances where an able executive is not only to be excused for breaking the letter of his promises, but must do so.

But what of the argument that the President has flouted the Constitution? It required a peculiar twist of logic to blame the President for the Supreme Court decisions, and to say that he is violating his oath because one group of Supreme Court justices, which happens to be the majority, has said that a particular measure does not fit its interpretation of the Constitution, while another group of the Court says the opposite. Since constitutionality is a legal question, and one which can only be decided on the basis of the interpretations of a small group of men who frequently differ among themselves, the President is certainly following his oath when he directs that Congress draft legislation to the best of its ability, concentrating on the needs of the particular situation, and leaving the determination of constitutionality to the Supreme Court. If Congress were to pass only legislation about which there was no doubt, we could have little use for the Supreme Court as the final arbiter of constitutional power. The Court would have nothing to consider.

Constitutional law is outside my line, but lawyers of great reputation tell me that the cases of other years furnish precedents which would justify a decision on either side of almost every constitutional issue. I am also informed that in 1934, by a five to four decision, the Supreme Court reversed a decision of Chief Justice Taney which had been handed down in

1843 and which until lately had been generally regarded as settled law. Constitutional law really means what the Judges have most recently decided.

Nevertheless, this has been one of the chief arguments of the critics of the New Deal. They kept quiet for almost two years, but with the Supreme Court's first decision against the New Deal, they thought they saw a safe way of attacking the administration without antagonizing its beneficiaries: the farmers, the working men, the youth, the majority of home-owners, and the majority of small business men—that is, the people of the United States.

The New Deal cannot be generally condemned, because its merits and achievements are a matter of record. But to show conflicts with the printed word, the party document, the Constitution, or the Ten Commandments—that was a new idea, and a very easy one to follow, because disparities can always be found in two documents, even if written by the same man. It was also a very desirable thing to do because it obviated the need for real analysis and real criticism.

So there was let loose a mammoth of propaganda, not against the merits or demerits of the New Deal, its achievements and what it failed to achieve, its real costs and profits, but against the fact that it does not conform to document 1, 2 or 3. But the man in the street, after he has heard that the New Deal does not conform to this, that, or the other, that it is an attempt to create a socialistic dictatorship, that it is ruining the nation and destroying the government credit, that it is dishonest, and what not, will still want somebody to tell him whether or not it is not good, whether he is safer and more prosperous with it or without it. These questions the critics do not answer.

But to the man in the street, the answers are obvious. He cannot take seriously this parade of imaginary horribles—for the simple reasons that the so-called "socialistic dictatorship" of President Roosevelt has behaved in such an orthodox manner that nobody noticed its presence except hysterical critics; that the country's "ruin" is reflected in a practical return to the average production of 1923–1925; and that the "ruined" government credit is reflected in the government's being able to borrow at rates never known in history.

We are apt to become somewhat sentimental and sympathetic when our earthly possessions are in danger, and may even begin to believe in planning and other such "superstitions." This was the situation of many of our leading "rugged individualists" of 1936 as their silence of 1933 so vividly indicated.

Quiet was Mr. Hoover; silent was former Secretary Mills; and scarcely a sound was uttered by many of the others who have since started to "write and talk continuously" as the apostles of the anti-Roosevelt movement. At that time some of the now most vocal critics of the New Deal bit their lips, hoping against hope that perhaps, by some trick, President Roosevelt would succeed in bringing economic order out of chaos, and they were, to some extent, for him, or at least not antagonistic to him. But, as President Roosevelt continued to move on and clear up the jungle, as it became apparent that his acts were not to be just a sop to the masses, they acquired a new feeling of confidence and self-assurance based on improved property values and the stimulus of recovered treasures. They steadied their nerves, found their voices, and fell back into their places in the ranks of the "Old Deal."

In 1933, after the election was over and they appreciated Mr. Roosevelt's great appeal to the people of the nation, they saw some justification and use for the President's talents of "showmanship." But in 1935 when these same gentlemen definitely began to feel they were out of danger these talents became in their minds a definite "menace" to the well-being of the country (the country, of course, means them).

If we are to piece together the attitudes of this group, it appears that, 1932 and 1933, when the country was threatened with a complete breakdown and when President Hoover lost control over Congress and didn't appeal to the imagination of the people, it was useful to have a Roosevelt who had the confidence of the masses and could keep them from attempting more radical things than the New Deal. But these men, who were first for and are now against the President, hoped that when the country recovered it would not remember it had wanted any reforms and that President Roosevelt in 1935 would scrap the New Deal—relief, public works, agricultural policies, social security, stock exchange regulations, deposit insurance, etc.

These were their hopes but the President has continued to keep his promises and that has been embarrassing to them. It is the loyalty of the President to his own promises and to the people to whom these promises were made that, in 1935, caused these—who appreciate very little the virtues of consistency and loyalty, and who dared not say anything against the New Deal during the tragic days of 1933—to venture at last to oppose so vehemently the New Deal and the President.

Conclusion

I HAVE not attempted an appraisal of all the controversial problems faced by the administration and all their attempted solutions, because such an effort would require a volume far larger in scope than this small effort of mine was intended to be. Against many of the attempted remedies and administrative methods used by the President there can be leveled justifiable criticism, but as I have said before criticism of method should not be allowed to obscure the deserving quality of the Presidential objectives. And most of the criticism of the administration has been ineffective because it has been so sweeping, so indiscriminating, so thoroughly denunciatory.

In the field of relief, which involves so intimately the important problem of economy in government, the President has been forced to make decisions without the guidance of precedents from other years. No previous national administration in this country was faced with the problem of satisfying the primitive wants of our citizens. This assumption by the Federal Government of the responsibility for the creature welfare of millions of our people was not a goal of the President in the sense that there were alternatives. He did not actively seek to assume this burden or to take it away from states and municipalities. Federal intervention became an accomplished fact regardless of the President's volition. It would have been a Federal problem regardless of the man who entered the White House and despite his particular political, economic or social views. The dependence on Washington of the Kansas State Government for relief of the 1936 drought ironically and triumphantly establishes that.

Where is there offered a definite program in challenge of the Presidential policies? I do not mean general statements about liberty or states' rights. These will not suffice. We have had an avalanche of platitudes from those who criticize, but not a word of definite proposal. There is no thoughtful observer possessed of simple honesty who will deny that it has become (and inevitably so) the national government's duty to deal with the crisis and to adopt preventive methods in so far as the orderly constitutional processes will permit. To this pressing emergency the President has brought all his energy and enthusiasm. That his legislative program has in part foundered because not enough Supreme Court Justices could find basic law for it is, at the worst, but a critical commentary on his powers of divination. At best it represents a courageous attempt to test the oft-repeated dogma that the Constitution is a living organism, adequate to meet the needs of changing society.

The maintenance of the Democratic ideal, particularly in days of great economic suffering, demands regulation. The President's record is one of respect for individual rights and regard for the need of social control to handle that form of individualism which, unrestrained, destroys democracy.

My faith in Roosevelt and my belief in the ultimate triumph and broad benefit of his principles is much affected by my position as the father of a large family. Out of a chaotic condition which stunned everybody, out of a collapse which threatened the welfare of all of us, our nation has come to a relatively prosperous and harmonious era. The activities of the President, his courage, his leadership, his willingness to act, his legislative accomplishments are responsible for this happier and friendlier state of society. This the President has done without compromising one iota the time-honored safeguards of American liberty and orderly government. It is ingenious of the opposition to cartoon the President as a swashbuckling dictator riding roughshod over the liberties of our people. But where is the evidence? Challenge these critics to produce a single instance of executive disregard of the oath of his office. They will by that challenge be silenced.

The very breadth of his program for the America of the future postpones final judgment on each and every phase of the President's plan. Recovery we have had, and a goodly measure of it, at a cost not out of proportion to the beneficial results.

President Roosevelt, without impeding honest business, has imposed reasonable checks on avarice and greed which were so much responsible for our economic failure.

He has succeeded in his program of fundamental rehabilitation regardless of the enmities he has made and the opposition he has generated. Rescued from the quicksands of depression many of us, now that we feel the solid ground of recovery under our feet, forget to give thanks. Nation-wide initiative stimulates and vitalizes life whereas before there was only helplessness. Who among us, given the choice, would return to the terror of 1933 or step backward from the sound threshold of the future into the economic quicksand of the year before the New Deal?

Appendix A

Total Revenues and Expenditures of United
States Treasury—Fiscal Years 1929–1936*
(Millions of Dollars)

	Total Ordinary Receipts and Postal Revenues	Total Ordinary and Postal Expenditures	Deficit
1929	$4,730	$4,536	194[5]
1930	4,883	4,706	177[5]
1931	3,974	4,877	903
1932	2,709	5,865	3,156
1933	2,826	5,889	3,063
1934	3,864[1]	7,822	3,958[1]
1935	4,661[2]	7,745[3]	3,084[2]
1936	5,000	9,400	4,400[4]

* Pp. 323–327, Report of Secretary of the Treasury
for 1935; for 1936, Daily Treasury Statements and Estimated
Postal Revenues and Expenses.

[1] Exclusive of $2,811,376,000 increment resulting from
reduction in the weight of the gold dollar.

[2] Exclusive of $1,738,020 increment resulting from re-
duction in weight of gold dollar and $140,111,441.47
seigniorage.

[3] Exclusive of $113,022,629 chargeable against incre-
ment on gold.

[4] Including about $1,700,000,000 for payment of adjusted
service certificates.

[5] Surplus.

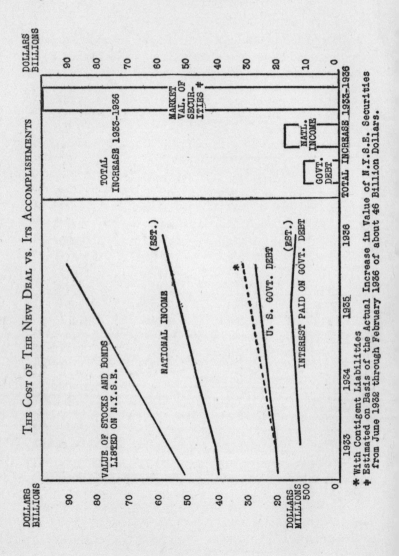

THE COST OF THE NEW DEAL vs. ITS ACCOMPLISHMENTS

* With Contingent Liabilities

✠ Estimated on Basis of the Actual Increase in Value of N.Y.S.E. Securities
  from June 1932 through February 1936 of about 46 Billion Dollars.

The cost of the New Deal's attack against the depression is illustrated by the government deficits which, since 1932, have totaled about $14,500,000,000 (including payments for Veterans' Bonus).

TOTAL PUBLIC DEBT OF THE UNITED STATES*

(End of Month)	Gross	Net
1929 February	$17,345,496,893.54	$17,378,514,363.60
June	16,931,197,747.60	16,742,754,739.67
1933 February	20,934,728,350.43	20,858,055,565.92
June	22,538,672,163.90	21,834,564,893.36
1936 February	30,519,622,339.63	29,531,693,529.98
June	33,779,000,000.00	31,097,000,000.00[1]

Contingent Liabilities	
1936 April	$4,704,833,038.06

* Public Debt Statements of United States Treasury.
[1] Gross debt less balance in general fund.

The increased public debt of over $10,000,000,000 during the tenure of the administration, together with the increase in contingent liabilities of about $4,700,000,000 (a large portion of which is recoverable because of sound asset backing) illustrate the method of financing the cost of the New Deal's attack against the depression (to be reduced, however, by the increase of $2,000,000,000 in the stabilization fund).

NATIONAL INCOME 1929–1936[1]

($000,000)

	Produced	Paid Out
1929	$81,034	$78,632
1930	67,917	72,932
1931	53,584	61,704
1932	39,545	48,362
1933	41,742	44,940
1934	48,397	50,174
1935	52,959	53,587
1936	60,000[2]	

[1] Source: Survey of Current Business.
[2] Estimated.

National income has risen from a low of less than $40,000,000,000 in the year preceding Roosevelt's inauguration to about $53,000,000,000 last year and probably will be in the neighborhood of $60,000,000,000 this year. This means a recovery of about $20,000,000,000 during the President's term and recovery approaching the 1930 level.

MARKET VALUE OF SECURITIES LISTED ON NEW
YORK STOCK EXCHANGE

		Bonds		Stocks	
		Value $000,000	Average Price	Value $000,000	Average Price
As of end of					
May	1929	$47,297[1]	$95.98	$70,921	$76.07
	1930	48,489[1]	96.92	75,019	61.46
	1931	47,630[1]	93.67	42,534	32.58
	1932	36,857[1]	70.62	16,141	12.23
	1933	32,998	80.79	32,473	25.10
	1934	38,239	90.17	33,817	26.13
	1935	39,618	90.62	34,549	26.50
	1936	39,648	93.83	49,999	37.35

[1] Including United Kingdom 5% War Loan 1929–1947
stricken December 1932.

These series indicate the increase in market values which
has taken place since February, 1933. The value of stocks
on the New York Stock Exchange, adjusted for listings and
delistings, has risen over $30 billions, and similarly bonds
may be estimated to have risen over $9 billions. This is
merely a sample of the whole rise in value of securities,
commodities, and other property.

INDEXES OF EMPLOYMENT AND PAYROLLS*

		Factory	
		Employment	Payrolls
Monthly Average	1929	104.8	109.1
	1930	91.5	88.7
	1931	77.4	67.5
	1932	64.1	46.1
	1933	69.0	48.5
	1934	78.8	61.9
	1935	82.2	70.3
	1936	84.2[1]	75.8
May	1929	105	113
	1930	95	95
	1931	80	73
	1932	63	47
	1933	63	43
	1934	83	67
	1935	81	69
	1936	86	79

* Bureau of Labor Statistics.
[1] First five months.

The basic nature of the decline prior to, and the recovery since Roosevelt are illustrated by these payroll and employment figures, the former rising over 90 per cent from January, 1933 to May, 1936, and the latter about 45 per cent.

INDUSTRIAL PRODUCTION*

1923–25 = 100

Year	Monthly Average	May Figures
1929	119	123
1930	96	102
1931	81	87
1932	65	60
1933	76	78
1934	79	86
1935	90	85
1936	99[1]	101

* Federal Reserve Board estimates.
[1] First five months.

As a broad measure of the recovery, the index of industrial production shows a rise from January, 1933 to May, 1936 of 59 per cent.

Auto Production and Registrations*
(000 omitted)

Production

| Year | Trucks and Passenger Cars | |
	Annual Totals	Month of May
1929	5,358	605
1930	3,356	420
1931	2,380	317
1932	1,369	184
1933	1,920	214
1934	2,779	330
1935	4,011	361
1936	2,037[1]	461

Registrations

| Year | Trucks and Passenger Cars | |
	Annual Totals	Month of May
1929	4,407	507
1930	3,036	388
1931	2,222	271
1932	1,277	150
1933	1,806	181
1934	2,292	259
1935	3,260	341
1936		455

* Survey of Current Business.
[1] First five months.

Production of automobiles (trucks and passenger cars) was higher in 1935 than in any year since 1929, and the first five months of 1936 show an increase of over 9 per cent above the corresponding period of 1935.

Building Contracts Awarded 37 States*
$000,000

Year	All Construction	
	Annual Totals	Month of May
1929	5,748	588
1930	4,524	457
1931	3,096	306
1932	1,356	146
1933	1,260	77
1934	1,548	134
1935	1,848	127
1936	997[1]	216

Year	Residential	Public Utilities	Public Works	Other
1929	1,915	524	935	2,374
1930	1,102	701	964	1,757
1931	811	295	876	1,114
1932	280	76	515	485
1933	260	103	499	398
1934	248	126	625	549
1935	479	112	578	679
1936[1]	260	85	241	111

* F. W. Dodge Reports.
[1] First five months.

The improvement in this basic industry is indicated by the increase in contracts awarded to the highest annual total since 1931, and the first five months of 1936 show a gain of 80 per cent over the corresponding period of 1935. While some of this improvement has resulted from public works, its basic character is illustrated by the increase in residential and other non-governmental construction.

IRON AND STEEL*
Production (ooo of Long Tons)

Year	Pig Iron		Steel Ingots	
	Annual Total	May	Annual Total	May
1929	42,288	3,898	54,312	5,286
1930	31,404	3,233	39,288	3,983
1931	18,276	1,994	25,194	2,552
1932	8,688	784	13,320	1,125
1933	13,212	887	22,596	1,976
1934	15,912	2,043	25,596	3,399
1935	21,012	1,727	33,418	2,634
1936	10,942[1]	2,648	17,341[1]	4,046

Steel Ingot Activity as Per Cent. of Capacity

Year	Annual Average	Average for May
1929	89	100
1930	63	74
1931	38	46
1932	20	20
1933	34	34
1934	37	57
1935	49	44
1936	61[1]	71

* Survey of Current Business.
[1] First five months.

Iron and steel, basic heavy industries, have shown gains in production so great that the rate of operations for the first five months of 1936 is greater than any year since and almost equals that of 1930.

CARLOADING*
(ooo Cars)
Monthly Averages

Year	Total	Coal	Merchandise LCL	Miscellaneous
1929	4402	758	1100	1712
1930	3823	661	1017	1473
1931	3106	544	914	1158
1932	2348	445	756	820
1933	2435	475	704	866
1934	2565	507	687	955
1935	2627	512	677	1020
1936[1]	2761	584	672	1090

Average Weekly Basis

May	Total	Coal	Merchandise LCL	Miscellaneous
1929	1052	157	264	414
1930	913	136	240	360
1931	740	114	218	295
1932	522	75	182	195
1933	536	81	166	203
1934	612	108	165	242
1935	582	98	160	229
1936	670	111	155	279

* Association of American Railroads.
[1] First five months.

Total carloadings show the effect of rising activity in all industries. For May, 1936, the total shows an increase of considerably more than 25 per cent over the equivalent 1932

PRICES OF ACTIVELY TRADED COMMODITIES*

		Wheat (Weighted Average, Six Markets, all Grades) $ per bushel	Cotton (Wholesale, Middling, N. Y.) $ per pound
Monthly Average	1929	1.21	.191
	1930	.87	.136
	1931	.63	.086
	1932	.55	.064
	1933	.75	.087
	1934	1.01	.124
	1935	1.04	.119
	1936[1]	.99	.116
May	1929	1.01	.195
	1930	1.01	.164
	1931	.76	.093
	1932	.61	.057
	1933	.73	.086
	1934	.94	.114
	1935	1.08	.123
	1936	.90	.117

* Survey of Current Business.
[1] First five months.

Improvement in prices of basic farm commodities, which are also important in the financial markets, is shown above, with wheat up almost 100 per cent from 1932 to 1935, and cotton up just about that much. The rise from the lows was greater.

NET INCOME OF ALL U. S. CORPORATIONS FILING INCOME TAX RETURNS
1929 – 1935

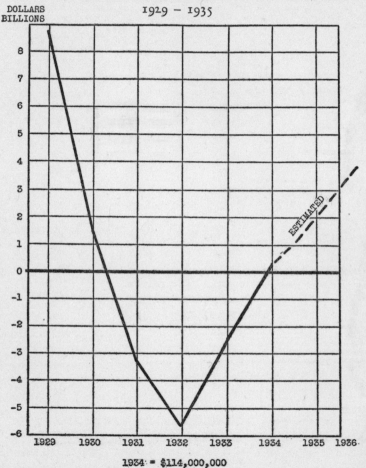

1934 = $114,000,000

INDEX

★

INDEX